sex and the city
plotholes

© 2020 N Taylor. All rights reserved.
ISBN 978-0-6488642-0-2

Contents

Season 1	7
Season 2	28
Season 3	62
Season 4	102
Season 5	139
Season 6	158

Having watched all the episodes I was amazed by how many 'plotholes' the author managed to uncover. Her observations are very insightful and we really get to know each SATC's characteristics: Samantha's sex addiction (although all the SATC girls have an abundance of sexual exploits immediately after snaring their prey); Carrie's material extravagances and personal insecurities; the intelligent Miranda's harsh black & white attitude to life; Charlotte's vacillation between extreme naivety and clever manipulation to get what she wants. For devoted SATC fans this hilarious and uplifting book is a must!

Lynda Cabeldu, First Time Literary Critic

I've never watched this tawdry show and indeed I never will; but this book was undeniably hilarious.

Lori Lebow, SATC Virgin

SATC is my religion, so I'm offended by this book. But fuck, it's funny.

Dario Holley, Gay Icon

Season 1

1 "Sex and the City"

We meet the four SATC thirty-something girls – Carrie, Charlotte, Miranda and Samantha. It could be said that SATC was the birth of many maxims, including the term "thirty-something". Here, Miranda celebrates her thirty-something birthday, while Mr Big makes his first appearance. We hear a few anecdotes about being a thirty-something woman in New York in the 90s.

An introduction to the four mixed personalities that are the SATC girls. It's a bit like meeting The Golden Girls 30 years before they were The Golden Girls – Dorothy Zbornak (Carrie), Sophia Petrillo (Miranda), Rose Nylund (Charlotte) and of course Blanche Devereaux (Samantha).

Some things to ponder as we head into the series: how does Carrie afford a beautiful Manhattan apartment, regular café dining and 100 pairs of $400 shoes when her only income appears to be writing a weekly column for a newspaper? Why, when in a later episode where Carrie introduces Mr Big to Samantha, do both of them conveniently forget that in this first episode, Samantha came onto him like a dog on a sausage sandwich, and he turned her down? Why is it that in six seasons of SATC, we only meet two other direct family members of the SATC girls (Miranda's sister, Charlotte's brother) and they get a total of 13 minutes of screen time? (I won't include Charlotte's father who spent 20 seconds giving her away at her first wedding, and didn't exchange a word with anyone). Finally, how many men do we expect Samantha to have sex with over the course of the series? It's like one of those jellybean counting competitions, without the jellybeans or the jar.

Special Note: The first episode is presented in a kind of mockumentary style, with rhetorical questions-to-camera, vox pops from the random public, and subtitles. The only one of these styles that remained by the end of the series was the ever-present voiceover, always from Carrie. Get used to hearing "I couldn't help but wonder...", the single most overused phrase in the series. It's like Seinfeld's "not that there's anything wrong with that". Except without the humour.

2 "Models and Mortals"

Miranda and Skipper, SATC's resident puppy-dog man, get together. Carrie meets Barkley, a man who only sleeps with models (and secretly videotapes himself having sex with them then broadcasts these videos to other people. None of this would wash twenty years onwards). Samantha tries to pretend to be a model so she can be taped too, but she's just kidding herself.

This episode explores the clichés about models: they purge their food, they starve themselves, they're loose, and they're stupid. Plus they seem to get all the men. One of the subtitled models earnestly tells the camera that she reads: sometimes, "I'll sit down and read a whole magazine from cover to cover". Another expresses the somewhat false statement that being beautiful will get you whatever you want. The tired old platitudes about models aren't even that funny in the 90s.

Despite the episode being a real downer on beautiful women, it appears that there are a few shallow men who only date beautiful women, even if it means they're punching above their weight. The SATC girls spend considerable time discussing how much they hate their body parts (I just yawned as I typed that) and how it's just not fair that models get their pick of all the shit men out there (the SATC girls should be grateful about that. I mean, if the point is that shit men go for models, then regular women wouldn't have to deal with them, would they?)

Like any demographic, models have their smart people too. Consider Elle MacPherson, Heidi Klum, Tyra Banks – all of whom have made fabulous careers out of doing a lot of stuff other than modelling.

I know that some people think it's fun to bitch about women who are super tall, thin and stunning. But can the models help it? Let them do their jobs. They have to eat too, despite popular opinion.

Meantime, Carrie finds herself at the apartment of a shallow greaseball named Barclay who tastelessly shows her his collection of explicit videos of himself having sex with models. And he doesn't just have one video going; there are at least seven of them, arranged in a sort of porn wall where all the TVs are stacked together like a Tetris game. Carrie is transfixed; she can't tear herself away, and even asks for a cigarette. If a guy I knew started showing me videos featuring himself like that, I'd find it a little gross. I think porn is best when it's anonymous. But maybe that's just me. I probably don't need to tell you that Samantha is the one who ends up sleeping with Barclay, and even begs him to film it. Watch out, Samantha, you don't know who's going to be watching that later. All I can say is, thank goodness this all happened before social media, otherwise Sam might have been reliving that one for decades.

Carrie bumps into Big (what a coincidence) at the afterparty for a fashion show and he shows her the model he's dating (what a coincidence).

3 "Bay of Married Pigs"

Carrie stays with "perfect couple" Patience and Peter at their Hamptons house, where they encourage Carrie to regale them with all her latest sexual exploits. In the morning she bumps into Peter, wandering about naked from the penis down. Carrie is clumsily introduced to Sean, friend of some friends, during an obvious set up attempt. Miranda is mistaken for a lesbian at work and is also set up, but with another woman. Samantha gets shitfaced. Charlotte gives us early insight into the WASP lifestyle, her natural modus operandi.

This episode is all about married vs single people, with a specific focus on an alleged war between the two that the single people must fight back (to win what I'm not sure). Carrie finds herself uncomfortably in the middle of perfect marrieds Peter and Patience, after getting a very good view of Peter's penis after he puts it on show for her. Patience is naturally furious and gets Carrie out of their house pronto so the marrieds can presumably have a big jolly fight about it.

Stanford comes back for his second appearance; he is the token gay, and a recurring and welcome relief from the female angst which inexorably makes its presence felt in every episode. Stanford and Carrie run into Carrie's ex who's now married to another guy. They hand Carrie a business card and tell her they'd love it if she would consider donating her eggs to them so they can have a baby. Because it's New York in the 90s and everyone does that – asks at random, in the street, a question filled with moral and ethical dilemmas, to someone they barely know. It's both flattering but also insulting at the same time, like they don't even care who Carrie is as long as she has eggs. Stanford wisely throws the card into the bin, thank goodness. This was a plotline best left alone.

Miranda is mistaken for a lesbian, and good for her – she is far from insulted, instead choosing to use the error as a way into the big league at work. She even ponders if it would be easier to just be a lesbian and goes for a kiss with her lesbian date, but this is all they need for both of them to realise that it wouldn't work. Not sure how kissing a woman would be so much different from kissing a man, so it makes you wonder if Miranda isn't just a bad kisser in general.

While Miranda is out on her faux-lesbian date, the other three attend a party at the home of Carrie's new man, Sean. When they arrive, they are all horrified to see that the party is comprised of couples only. (We've all been there, right.) Samantha deals with the situation by getting white-girl-wasted on tequila (very mature) and starts getting vocal, loud and embarrassing.

So Charlotte drags tanked-up Samantha back to Charlotte's apartment for the night, like she's 12 years old. However, Samantha isn't drunk enough to fall into bed and wake with a giant hangover. Instead she works out how to ride the lift back down to the ground floor so she can seduce the doorman back up to Charlotte's apartment and have sex with him. When Charlotte discovers what's going on, she is horrified. What did she expect? It's Samantha, after all. Should have just put her in a cab to her own joint, yes?

Carrie passes off her new man to Charlotte, after he's made it clear that he is desperate for marriage, children and domestic life, a massive turnoff for Carrie. Charlotte is up for all of that, but she is forced to dump the guy immediately when it appears his taste in crockery is not the same as Charlotte's. Of all the crazy-ass reasons to dump someone, this absolutely has to win. Even Seinfeld might have found this one a little bit fucking nutso.

4 "Valley of the Twenty-Something Guys"

75% of the SATC girls find themselves dating younger men – what a coincidence. In other coincidences, Carrie keeps bumping into Big, which in New York, a city of over 7 million people, isn't really that unlikely. Charlotte tries to figure out how to say no to anal sex, although Samantha tells her she should loosen up and just do it.

Unsurprisingly, each of the thirty-something girls is having trouble with their twenty-something (20-s) men. Samantha is horrified when hers points out that she has wrinkles on her neck. Carrie spends a night with her 20-s and wakes up to find that she is sleeping in a loft in what can only be described as a frat house, complete with filth, mess, no coffee, no toilet paper and freakish long-haired flatmates. It's almost as though she got into bed with a 17 year old, not a 26 year old.

Miranda is horrible to her 20-s, Skipper, as usual. It's a wonder he sticks around after he gets her the wrong drink at the bar and she reacts with predictable sarcasm. And Charlotte, dating a man who fits her only three criteria (looks, money and looks) is trying to figure out how to refuse anal sex with him. How about just saying "thanks but no"? Charlotte, you *run an art gallery.* You're in control of a business, making important decisions with important people all day long. Why make panic calls to your girlfriends and end up in a conference in the back of a cab, discussing it within earshot of the cab driver? And how is it legal to seat four people in the back of a cab? Samantha has of course already been the Up The Butt Girl, probably many times, so recommends it to Charlotte. Miranda, in an attempt to appear knowledgeable and valued in the conversation, just says something obscure about a power shift in the relationship. Thanks, Miranda. Not helpful.

Carrie goes on a "thing" (it's not a date, ok?) with Big and he brings along his boring, miserable friend. What a rude thing to do. Carrie reacts in the only way she knows how, ie. runs off and has sex with her 20-s. The episode ends with Carrie wandering down the street in what I hope is a fake trashy fur coat, looking like she's doing the walk of shame, when she *surprise!* sees Big yet again. It's just such a coincidence.

5 "The Power of Female Sex"

Carrie lets a female acquaintance Amalita buy her a new pair of shoes with Amalita's boyfriend's money (we can't call Amalita a friend of Carrie's. They've only met a few times and we never see Amalita again after this episode). Even though the title of the episode is "The Power

of Female Sex" we are given the strong impression that the Power does not lie in womens' ability to be smart, problem-solving, leaders, educators or any other respectable sort of attribute. It's really just about conning men for money. This episode is mostly devoted to reminding us how broke Carrie is.

Carrie goes out on the town with the gorgeous Amalita, a woman with some kind of European accent who makes her living shamelessly off very wealthy men who shower her with gifts, holidays, meals and money. Miranda refers to her as a "hooker with a passport", which has to be one of the funniest things she's ever said. When Carrie spends overnight in an expensive hotel with Gilles, a friend of Amalita's latest client (we assume) she is offended when he's left her $1,000 in an envelope the next morning when she wakes up.

Horrified and ashamed, Carrie nevertheless invites her friends to the hotel before she checks out so they can all shamelessly freeload and sample the delicious salmon room service. She complains that Gilles treated her like a hooker. Carrie: you slept in a hotel with a friend of your international callgirl/escort friend, whom you just met. You just treated *yourself* like a hooker. $1,000? You should be delighted. It could be a whole new career for you.

Meanwhile, Charlotte visits a painter whose work she desperately wants to exhibit. He's painting a series called "The Cunt" which is a collection of enormous and thankfully abstract paintings of cunts. He wants to paint Charlotte's. Charlotte was terrified he was going to ask her to sleep with him to get to his paintings. I think this is worse. Nevertheless, she agrees to do it (this is the same girl who wouldn't let her dream man go up her butt).

The girls ask Charlotte which of the paintings is her cunt, and she tells them. They stare at it in wonder. But how would they know if she's telling the truth? They could be candle flames, or tunnels, or orchids, or Aladdin's Cave. Also, they all look the same.

Miranda Quote: Carrie wondering what about her screams "whore" and Miranda saying "besides the $1,000 on the end table?"

6 "Secret Sex"

Carrie earns a free dress by agreeing to wear it and be photographed in it to appear on the side of a bus. I would have preferred the money (am I the only one who thinks this dress is fifty kinds of hideous?) Carrie then wears this hideous dress to her first proper date with Mr. Big, thus setting off the next five and a half seasons of angst about Mr Big. Miranda sleeps with a sports doctor, Ted, but can't help herself once in his apartment alone and searches through all his private stuff, finding a spanking-porn video in the process.

Miranda makes a classic mistake here. Think about it: if you discovered a dirty little secret about someone you were dating, assuming it didn't bother you, would you jokingly drop it into a conversation with them? Or would you shut up about it, in case it made things very awkward between you, as it did with Miranda and Ted in this case? I'm going to go with the latter. Miranda is the smart SATC girl – she's a partner in a law firm – so she should have had enough common sense to let her new man bring up his spanking fetish in his own good time, if at all. Better yet, she should have just introduced the spanking thing at their next bedtime session, like Samantha would have done. Tread carefully next time, Miranda. And stop snooping through people's stuff. It's not nice.

Now, onto Carrie's dilemma of the episode. To be fair, I would be quite annoyed if a guy took me back to the same restaurant on a second date, unless he'd asked me where I wanted to go and I had specifically said "please! Take me back to that awesome Szechuan restaurant. It's the best one I've ever been to and I want to try a whole bunch of different menu items this time!" But he didn't ask Carrie, and she didn't say that, so I get her confusion and disappointment. It's a bit like that Seinfeld episode where Jerry's girlfriend wears the same dress to every date.

Then there's Mike, the guy who dates this pretty girl Libby who's great in bed and has a proper job and just generally seems really sweet. Except he doesn't really "date" her – he's just using her as a fuck buddy and it's not clear whether Libby even gets that. Carrie misses a great opportunity to tell him what a total penis he's being, instead using the experience as fodder for her column (stuff about how some people sleep with people they're embarrassed about). He's perfectly entitled to sleep with someone he doesn't really like, of course. But to be ashamed enough to take them to a restaurant where there is little chance of being seen with her, and then refusing to introduce Libby to Carrie because he's so embarrassed by being in Libby's company? We never see Mike again, which suits me. What a tool.

7 "The Monogamists"

Carrie is berated by her friends for dumping them in favour of Mr Big, and makes it clear that she's only going out with the girls for dinner because Big is busy (turns out, busy on a date with another woman). Charlotte finds the perfect man, except for one thing: he expects blow jobs. Samantha is looking for an apartment, and is sprung about to have sex in one with her realtor. We get the first of many showings of her breasts. Miranda ruins Skipper's new relationship.

Miranda sees Skipper with a new girlfriend: a successful, pretty girl who works at *Vogue*. She's insanely jealous, even though Miranda was the one who broke it off with Skipper. (I need this explained to me, please). Miranda calls Skipper straight away and asks him out for a drink, which he agrees to, and they end up having sex. Let's dissect this:

- Miranda knew Skipper was dating someone
- She calls him for a drink and they have sex, even though she knew he was seeing someone
- He tells her he's already broken up with the other beautiful girl in favour of Miranda, and Miranda responds by telling him he "didn't have to do that"

I'm searching for the right words to describe this twisted, thoughtless, illogical situation but I can't find them. Miranda can't leave Skipper alone, can she: she deliberately makes him cheat on his new girlfriend (she didn't know at this point that they had broken up), she knows how much he adores her and uses that fact to get a free screw with no intention of getting back together with him, and then becomes annoyed when Skipper is upset with how things have proceeded. Where's your head at, Miranda? I'm shaking mine.

Regarding Charlotte, well, I feel like I'm back in high school here, too. Charlotte has a list of things she will and won't do in bed, and I guess she's entitled to that. But in case we haven't already noted before, Charlotte can be a bit contrary about these things. She's letting people paint her cunt. In future episodes she'll let guys lick her ring and consider threesomes. But she won't suck a little cock? And as for her boyfriend Michael, he shouldn't really have made such a big deal about not getting any head. Doesn't he realise that whoever he marries, he won't be getting any after the wedding in any case?

Let's move onto Carrie. She's very annoyed when she discovers that Big is dating other women, and so she should be. She uses the situation to discuss monogamy and its pros and cons in her column, so at least it's provided her with some material. In an attempt to make it up to her, Big makes things so much worse by taking her to a posh party with his posh friends where Carrie is treated to a round of awkward moments between Big's ex and his male friends, who allude to Big as being a bit promiscuous. This comes as a surprise to Carrie and she storms off. It's their second (or is it third) fight in two episodes. We're just getting started.

We are also treated to a round of vox pops from random people explaining their definitions of monogamy and why it works for them (eg. it's great because you can still see prostitutes on the side and if you're a woman, you don't have to shave your legs). It's good that these little snippets disappear from the show eventually, because they are terribly annoying.

Questionable Plotline: Zero points to Skipper, who not only answers the phone while having sex with his girlfriend, but then breaks it off with her while he's still inside her. Who does that?

8 "Three's a Crowd"

It's threesome week, yay! Charlotte has found yet another cute, sexy man and this one wants a threesome, which Charlotte agrees to. (Just for reference, I refer you to the last ep, where Charlotte wouldn't give blow jobs.) In a startling coincidence, Carrie finds out that Big had a threesome once and it was with his ex-wife, who has also remained a secret until now. Miranda is annoyed that none of her friends will pretend they'd have a threesome with her, so she answers an ad in the paper from a couple looking for a third wheel. Samantha is also offered a threesome, from the wife of the married man she's banging (ecchhhh!)

Carrie feels enormously threatened upon hearing that Big has an ex wife who he did threesomes with, so she makes an appointment to pitch a book idea with Big's ex who happens to be…. a publisher. And Carrie is a writer! What a coincidence. So Carrie sits down in front of this woman who doesn't know that Carrie is seeing her ex husband, and is asked what she is pitching.

Turns out Big's ex, Barbara, only publishes children's books (whoops! Nice research there, Carrie) so Carrie is put on the spot. Showing a vast lack of imagination and no idea about children, Carrie mumbles on about Little Cathy who smokes magic cigarettes. Come on, Carrie. Surely you could have done so much better. Even more unrealistically, Barbara later invites Carrie to lunch (why?) and tells her that her idea isn't really appropriate. Surely Barbara could have conveyed that in a phone call.

Charlotte is flattered into the idea of a threesome by her new man Jack, who suggests they find another woman pronto. Samantha warns her that the only way to do a threesome properly is to be the guest star, not the one in the relationship. Charlotte, Samantha and Carrie then have a warm loving conversation about how they'd all threeway it with each other, and Miranda is left out in the cold. Personally I'd be glad about that but Miranda finds it insulting and responds by lining up a date with a couple from Craigslist or something, and wastes their evening by running out of the date once she's ascertained that they'd do a threesome with her. I dunno... it seems like a shit tonne of effort to go to, just to make sure there's someone who'd do a threesome with you. I can think of a few hundred things I'd rather be doing with my spare time.

But back to Charlotte and her man Jack, who are at a masked ball together, looking for a woman to hook up with them. Apparently all it takes is for Charlotte to wink at a girl, and there they are, in a bedroom upstairs at the ball. And of course Jack leaps on the new girl, literally squeezing Charlotte out of the way and out the door so he can get it on with her. Apparently, it seems Jack didn't really want a threesome. He just wanted to sleep with someone else with Charlotte's permission. Charlotte should have listened to Samantha after all.

9 "The Turtle and the Hare"

Big says he's never going to get married again (never say never, Mr Big). Carrie is devastated, despite not having even thought about the possibility. The adorable Stanford promises to marry Carrie in order to inherit a family fortune. (Do it, Carrie!) Samantha decides to work a fixer-upper on a man who she considers a blank enough canvas to bring up to her standards. Then there's a whole lot of stuff about vibrators.

The girls attend an expensive wedding of someone's friend Brooke, who although is always seen with the best of the best-looking men with money, has decided to settle for an ugly, rich man. You almost think to yourself, well maybe he has the most wonderful personality and she's not a gold digger, but then Brooke tells Carrie that it's better to marry someone who loves you more than you love them, and her cover is blown.

At the wedding, a guy called The Turtle makes a nuisance of himself by bothering the girls with his desperation and his bad breath. So it's kind of strange when Samantha bumps into him again while on a bad date (what a coincidence) and is sufficiently charmed by his compliment when she was feeling down that she decides to make him into her dream man. She throws him a facial, some new clothes, and presumably some mouthwash, but you can't get the turtle out of the man. He's still the same boring windbag.

Charlotte becomes addicted to a vibrator called the Rabbit and starts refusing to leave the house because she's suddenly discovered she doesn't need a man to have an orgasm. Carrie and Miranda storm the joint, toss the bedsheets aside and find the vibrator, whereupon Miranda *picks it up with her bare hands and puts it in her purse*. This is just too gross for words.

Best Quote: "You know, he is a fruit". From Stanford's Chanel wearing grandmother.

Second Best Quote: Big hilariously calling Carrie "Ms Blatch".

Miranda Moment: watch Miranda when she wishes the bride all the best with a big grin, and then the look just slides off to reveal her usual resting bitch face. Tee hee.

10 "The Baby Shower"

The SATC girls are invited to their friend Laney's baby shower. Charlotte is the only one who has any concept of what is a suitable gift for a pregnant woman. Carrie thinks she might be pregnant but is too gutless to just take a test already. Samantha is so appalled that people are still getting married and having babies that she throws an "I Don't Have a Baby!" party. People actually attend it.

The absolute worst thing about this episode is the vox pops from the party attendees; all mothers who tell us very weird things about their lives: one is secretly a lesbian, one has an internet lover, and another sadly remembers her previous life before losing all her corporate power to have children. It's a blatant attempt to assert that having a marriage and a baby is soul-destroying and life-sucking. Subtle.

Laney, who was once a life-of-the-party girl who never hesitated to show everyone her tits, has settled down in a lovely suburban house and quite frankly the SATC girls are disgusted. Well, not Charlotte, because Laney is living her dream, including naming her first child using Charlotte's own chosen baby name. Charlotte makes a huge thing out of this — accusing Laney of stealing "her" baby name. But baby names aren't copyright, and Laney isn't exactly a huge part of Charlotte's life anyway, so why get so upset? It's a poxy, anaemic name anyway — "Shayla" — ick! It sounds like a brand of mattress. Charlotte is acting like she's in school and someone purchased the last strawberry lollipop from the canteen. Samantha uses the situation to inflame things further by insulting Laney rudely, calling her a bitch, at *her own baby shower*. Way to behave, Samantha.

Laney then calls Carrie to reminisce about the party and longingly express the desire to invite herself to Samantha's I Don't Have A Baby! party. Does she not remember how Charlotte and Samantha were so breathtakingly bad-mannered to her? It was five minutes ago.

Laney then crashes Samantha's party, to the further disgust of Samantha and Charlotte. Laney gets drunk, even though she's pregnant, and then fails at showing everyone her party trick (her tits) because she can't get her maternity top off. But seriously: who wears a maternity top when they're pregnant? Aren't maternity tops for breastfeeding? Women don't strap themselves into those things until they've *had* the baby.

Carrie bundles a very sad and sorry Laney into a cab to Connecticut, which is just under one hundred miles away. *One hundred miles*. How did Laney get to the party in the first place and how much was that cab fare?

Carrie discovers in the last scene of the episode that she isn't pregnant after all (don't you hate getting your period when you're walking down the street) and thus endeth the last 10 days of agonising about whether she'd be a good mother and wondering how to tell Big. All of which could have been avoided by peeing on a stick. Pfft.

Miranda Quote: after hearing a mother declare her son is a "god" and she tells him so every day, Miranda posits:

Q. "Thirty years from now, what do you think the chances are that some woman's gonna be able to make Andy happy?

A. I'm gonna go with zero."

Classic.

11 "The Drought"

Carrie has been dating Big for about three weeks now, and starts to worry that he's not interested in her any more because they're going to bed at night sometimes without having had sex in it first. Charlotte dates a man on Prozac who can't get it up. Miranda hasn't had sex for three months which seems to be a huge problem for some reason. Samantha becomes deeply attracted to her very odd yoga instructor, and is dismayed that he's celibate. She does her level best to persuade him to fuck her.

Someone should tell Carrie that frequency of the sex is one of the first things to ease off a bit as a relationship progresses – it's quite normal. Also, getting advice from someone like Samantha, who proclaims that something is very wrong with the relationship (like she'd know) is like getting advice from your cat about what to do with the dog.

I can't help but wonder if Carrie has ever dated anyone longer than a month, because if so, she would know this. Of course it didn't help that the easing off happens to coincide with a completely hilarious fart that Carrie makes as they're having a morning snuggle. I think we can all have a little cringe at how embarrassing that would be, but most of us would also forget about it soon enough, especially as Big was so understanding and compassionate about it (he warned Carrie not to go under the sheets afterwards. So sweet.)

But it's Carrie's fart, so an episode is contrived out of it. (This episode should have been called "The Fart".) The fart is discussed in detail with Miranda (who eventually tells Carrie to shut up about it already, it's boring her) and Samantha (who most unhelpfully admonishes Carrie for behaving like a human being in front of a man.) Carrie can't bring herself to discuss it around Charlotte, because we all know that Charlotte wouldn't even know what a fart was. But Carrie does ruminate upon the lack of sex with Big over the last 48 hours with each of the SATC girls like it's the end of the world, and Samantha offers her cheap solution, which is to throw herself at Big and make sure she doesn't leave him alone until she gets it. It's all in the timing though, which Samantha didn't emphasize properly. When you're giving advice to someone as neurotic as Carrie, you have to make sure she doesn't get it all confused and do it wrong.

Get it wrong she does, climbing all over Big and getting in his face while he's watching The Sport (Carrie! No, no no! I can't believe you aren't aware of this important rule about men. Don't interrupt The Sport). Big is annoyed, Carrie storms furiously out and we just know that Big won't get an apology. Don't we?

Meantime, Samantha is forced to give up her ideas of destroying her odd yoga teacher's celibacy, as she can't stand the sight of a hard cock when it isn't coming towards her. She picks up some other random guy at yoga instead. They actually run out of the yoga class together before it's finished. Come *on*.

Miranda is verbally sexually harassed by some hunky looking workman on the street doing something with concrete or paving or whatever, and because it's the closest thing she's had to sex for nearly 4 months now, she orders the guy to act upon his carefully chosen words and give it to her. He's terrified and starts to cry. Well, not quite but I have to say good on Miranda for calling the bluff of one of those aggressive stalking workmen. I was really impressed. I might try that trick one day myself.

Charlotte kisses and cuddles a guy for a few weeks before discovering that Carrie used to date him. That might be pretty distasteful to most, but Charlotte's ok with it and presses Carrie for information. She's both shocked but also thrilled to discover that the guy is a sex maniac, and assumes he's been holding it all in, to respect Charlotte's values (ie. no sex until you've had 144 dates). Armed with her new knowledge, Charlotte is crushed when she discovers the guy's not really holding his lust for her, he's just Prozac-impotent. And he won't give up the Prozac. That is all.

Back to Carrie. Big makes the first conciliatory move; which is, well, Big of him; seeing as Carrie was the one who ruined his night by acting all needy and irrational when he was trying to watch The Sport. They kiss and make up. For now.

12 "Oh Come All Ye Faithful"

Miranda dates a Catholic guy who is compelled to shower after sex. For some reason this annoys her. Is it because he's Catholic or does she hate too much showering because it's wasteful of water? Carrie decides to infiltrate Big's life by getting herself in front of his mother without Big's permission. Samantha falls in love (a rare event) but sadly the relationship can't survive due to the lack of Samantha's key requirement: a big cock. Charlotte is so desperate to find out if she'll ever meet the right man that she goes to a hokey tarot card reader to predict her future.

Charlotte is horrified when Samantha announces that she may have found The One That She'll Marry, so she acts quickly by consulting a crackpot ballgazer. Why is Charlotte getting all the stupid plotlines of late? It's a relief when Charlotte is sceptical enough to work out that the tarot card reader was just a crock telling her lies to ply more money out of her.

Why do people believe in this sort of voodoo? If Charlotte, a woman of moderate intelligence, can't figure out that future-predicting is a bust and if it was a precise science the world would be a much better place, then I guess she deserves the stupid plotlines.

Meantime, Miranda is continually offended when her guy, Thomas John, leaps out of bed right after shooting his load, every time, making her feel, well, dirty. Instead of just putting up with it/getting used to it, Miranda makes a big deal about it. Thomas John orders her out of his apartment and his life, explaining derisively that if he wants to let his Catholic guilt ruin a post coital snuggle then that's his problem. Miranda has already admitted to Carrie that she would never have dated a Catholic having known he was one, so I'm not sure why she sticks around after she discovers he is. A deal breaker is a deal breaker. But apparently not in this case.

Carrie is busily stalking a church on a Sunday morning, for column research purposes. By research I mean she is standing on the footpath gazing at the churchgoers finishing up their worship, wondering (I assume) if she can spot any physical differences between them and non-churchgoers. To her concern, she sees Big in the throng, all dressed up in a suit with an elegantly dressed older woman, who he is helping into a cab. The woman is his mother, and Carrie begs Big to take her to church too, so she can meet this mother of his. Big says absolutely not, and offers her a trip to the Caribbean instead. Take it, Carrie! But no, Carrie can't help herself, can she. She gets all frocked up and drags Miranda along to the next Sunday service, where she makes an exhibition of herself by dropping a bible from the upper level so it crashes to the floor with a noise like a gunshot. Awkward.

Big has no choice but to introduce Carrie to his mother (because there she is, in his face again like last episode) and his mother has clearly no recognition of who Carrie is. Big explains it's because he's introduced his mother to so many girlfriends that he's tired of doing it. It's the final straw for Carrie, and she ends the relationship right before a plane trip to the Caribbean. I guess that's better than ending it on the plane *to* the Caribbean.

Samantha discovers that her new love, the one she was going to marry, has a tiny penis, which is *her* deal breaker. It's the way she discovers this fact which is implausible: she doesn't know it's tiny until he puts it in her. Someone like Samantha likes to grab penises long before this stage. She'd usually try for a squeeze during a kiss, or when she was undressing him (which by the way didn't even happen because he's wearing a blue collared work shirt as he fucks her for the very first time), or she'd warm things up a little first with a bit of head. There must have been no foreplay whatsoever, and no touching. It looks like the worst fuck ever.

There is, however, one of the funniest SATC scenes ever to follow: the girls confront an anguished Samantha in the toilet stall at a party, where she confesses that her love has a gherkin dick that's only three inches when hard. The girls are sad and sympathetic but there's nothing they can do to help. Samantha has the good grace to feel like a bad person for being so shallow about it all, and to be honest you gotta feel for her. It is, as they say, disappointing.

10 Inappropriate/Silly SATC Wardrobe Choices

1. A matchy-matchy belt around your bare waist with a crop top and hipster skirt - *Carrie*
2. A Lindy Bop 50s skirt and stilettos to spend the weekend in your boyfriend's shed - *Carrie*
3. A fur coat that's trashy if it's real and trashy if it's not - *Carrie*
4. Hideous stilettos with pom poms (I don't even care if they are Manolos) - *Carrie*
5. The Naked Dress that was worn on the side of a bus, and to a date with Big, that was just a plain boring skin tone dress (also worn with #3) - *Carrie*
6. A sloppy hoodie with a silk skirt - *Miranda*
7. The cowgirl hat with the bandeau bra at a Hamptons Party - *Carrie*
8. A ruffled pink 80s prom dress with so much accessorising it's hard to know where to look - *Carrie*
9. Hotpants with hooker heels - *Carrie*
10. The pink shapeless puff tent worn to Bobby and Bitsy's wedding with the worst hairstyle ever seen on SATC - *Carrie*

Season 2

1 "Take Me Out to the Ballgame"

Carrie is mourning the loss of Big, and constantly worrying about seeing him by accident, which is annoying the other girls. They go to a baseball game, where Samantha compares the world's smallest wiener with her boyfriend's penis. Carrie chases after a Yankee and asks him out. Samantha stands gawking outside the men's changeroom which is full of naked men wandering around just inside the door. Charlotte has met the perfect guy (again) but he is a constant public ball-adjuster. Miranda goes completely spak when the girls can't talk about anything other than men, balls and penises.

This is the one episode where Miranda inexplicably finds the girls' dirty talk unacceptable and tries to steer the conversation to other more important things, like baseball regulations and her new palm pilot. Showing no patience or sympathy for Carrie's whining about Big (we can't really blame her there), she storms out of a café conversation with the SATC girls, but I'm not exactly sure who else she has to talk to. Don't worry: by next episode Miranda will be back on track with the trash talk.

Carrie goes out with her Yankee a couple of times, which initially upsets Miranda because Miranda is the baseball freak, not Carrie, who thinks baseball is kind of boring. Nevertheless the baseball guy is super cute and charming, but Carrie ends up crying in his mouth after she sees Big for real on their second date, thus ruining her chances with the "rebound guy". She also rather rudely tells him to go away, and when he won't, because he's concerned for her, she tells him she'll go away instead. The poor guy. He must have been so confused.

Samantha is still hanging around ~~her small penis~~ James, but uses every opportunity to moan about it. I think it's a race to see who can be most boring - Carrie or Samantha – but Miranda's in there too, banging about baseball rules and all the player names (no-one cares).

Charlotte's big problem is wardrobe malfunction etiquette: how long can she stand to be seen with a guy who's always adjusting his crotch? Samantha tries to get to the bottom of the issue (is it low-hanging fruit?) but as Charlotte still hasn't reached 144 dates it's impossible to determine why the guy might be so uncomfortable with his equipment. However, Charlotte thinks she has the answer: new underwear! Instead of being thrilled about this, her new man Paul is offended with his gift and by Charlotte, and orders her out of his life. I initially thought he was being pathetic and ungrateful, but then I wondered how I'd feel if a guy I hadn't slept with bought me new panties, even comfortable ones. And I have to say I see where Paul is going with this: I might be offended, pathetic and ungrateful too. But then maybe it really depends on how I felt about the guy. Tough call. The jury's out on this one.

2 "The Awful Truth"

Susan-Sharon, Carrie's friend, is married to one of the most awful men we'll ever see on SATC, and she tries to leave him but fails because she's too low in self-worth. Samantha finally finds a way to tell James that his penis is ruining their relationship. Miranda has a hard time talking dirty in bed (because that stuff's only reserved for trash talk with girlfriends). Charlotte gives up on men and buys a dog instead.

Firstly, we'll get Charlotte's dog out of the way. Charlotte made a big mistake here. Huge. How could she have not known that Laura Ashley and puppies do not go together? Here's what puppies do: they poo on rugs. They wee on beds. They scratch at expensive furniture, chew shoes and bark nonstop. I thought everyone knew this. Sadly, Charlotte found out the hard way that puppies are even more unreliable and more destructive than a man. Next time, Charlotte, get a really old dog. Or just a sugar daddy.

The main plot in this episode concerns Susan-Sharon (S-S, I can't be bothered typing all that again) and her sadistic, foul, abusive husband, who mistreats not just S-S in Carrie's presence but also Carrie herself. S-S gives Carrie a very expensive scarf for her birthday and Carrie asks straight away if she can return it for cash (huh? What a vulgar thing to say! Perhaps Carrie could have had some manners here?). Then Richard, S-S's husband, storms in and berates them for making noise, ordering Carrie out of the house, complete with use of the F word. What a charmer.

Carrie ponders whether the abusive behaviour was foreplay, precipitated by Carrie's presence. Does Carrie understand anything about domestic violence? Later, S-S asks Carrie for advice about whether she should leave Richard. And instead of being honest and telling her friend that Richard is an abusive arsewipe and she should get out now, Carrie just murmurs something non-committal because she's scared of copping the blame for the failure of the marriage.

I dunno. S-S is one of those one-episode friends who just show up for a brief blot on the SATC timeline. Carrie has nothing to lose by telling S-S to get out before she becomes a shell of her former self; a weeping, esteemless wreck unable to get through the day without having a mental breakdown because her train was late. Because that's what domestic violence can do to recipients of such abuse. When S-S does find the strength to land herself at Carrie's apartment as a marriage escapee, she wretchedly spends quite a lot of time thinking of Richard and how he's not that bad and why hasn't he called her. And who slaps her, and orders her to snap to out of it? No-one.

At the end of the episode, S-S does go back to Richard, and they adopt Charlotte's puppy so Richard can scream at it instead of S-S. There's a lot of unresolved stuff here that should have been left alone in the first place: dealing with domestic violence is a subject that needs to be done properly, or not at all.

James, he of gherkin penis, manages to convince Samantha to go to a therapist to discuss their appalling sex life, because somehow Samantha can't just make up an easy lie; by for example telling him she's in love with someone else. So they go to the world's most ineffective sex counsellor, who has no idea how to get to the root of the problem and instead advises them to "have fun" with sex and "play erotic games". It's so funny to watch someone telling of all people, Samantha, how to have sex. In the end Samantha cracks it and blurts out the real issue, which hurts James enormously (in contrast to his penis). That was $160 well spent on therapy. Next time, Samantha, tell a gentle lie. It'll still hurt but it'll be cheaper.

Finally, Miranda is schooled in the art of dirty talk, by Charlotte of all people. (Isn't this Samantha's job?) Charlotte sometimes can't say "s-e-x" out loud, but she sure can act all disapproving when Miranda admits she's uncomfy with dirty talk in bed. When Miranda does finally crack the dirty talk ice, all she can do is repeat the word "cock" and "hard" a few times before offending her man by pointing out how he loves her finger up his arse. And yay verily was thus the endeth of Miranda's dirty talk.

Best line: Samantha: "What can I say? I need a big dick."

$160 therapist: "I hear that."

3 "The Freak Show"

Charlotte is picked up at a party by Mr Pussy, a guy who likes to eat hors d'oeuvres in public like he's giving them head (it's gross). Carrie dates a succession of guys with apparent psychological issues. Samantha visits the doctor for the latest in anti-aging treatments. Miranda doesn't get up to terribly much.

Carrie has the trifecta of bad dates, and then she meets a fourth one who actually seems OK (for the record, that's quite a few dates in one episode.) But in traditional Carrie style, she lets this fourth one discover her in all her paranoid glory; in his apartment where he'd left her alone, riffling through all his stuff, making a big mess everywhere, and attempting to crack open a box that wasn't even locked. Carrie's behaviour on this occasion is just cringeworthy and possibly the stupidest display of paranoia even exhibited, even from Carrie.

Mr Pussy, meanwhile, goes down on Charlotte an unseemly number of times because that's all he's interested in. Literally. He appears to do nothing else but go down on hundreds of New York women and for some reason, even knowing this, Charlotte allows him to do the same to her before she finally tries to extract some sort of personality by regaling him with stories of how much she enjoyed summer camp. Admittedly this is not the most exciting of conversations to have, so Mr Pussy responds by trying to excite a fig and Charlotte sighs in defeat. There were quite a few empty-headed men on SATC but I'd give first prize to Mr Pussy for sure. (Second prize? Probably Trey. But we'll get to him later).

Samantha is confronted with an aging crisis, the first of several during the SATC series. She deals with this one by having her bum fat injected into her face. The whole procedure was precipitated by Samantha's last date guessing her age (somewhat correctly) as 40. Samantha was so annoyed by someone so accurately guessing her age that she turns down his offer of bondage, which is something she'd normally jump at. I hope he learned his lesson: age-guessing is a minefield, and it won't get you laid.

4 "They Shoot Single People, Don't They?

Carrie is given the chance to appear on the COVER of **New York Magazine,** *so she decides to stay up all night drinking and smoking because who needs beauty sleep for a major photoshoot? All the girls desperately try to prove that they're single and fabulous…. by quickly hooking up with as many men as they can. Miranda very unconvincingly fakes orgasms. Charlotte decides that she should marry a handyman, who can fix broken shit around her apartment. Samantha is wined, dined, flattered, "we'd" and eventually stood up by an oily knob called William.*

Take note: if you're being photographed, by anyone at all, for any reason, they might use a horrible photograph of you for their own evil purposes. In this case, a major magazine in New York chose to use an ugly test shot of Carrie's hungover, sleepless, sheet-creased and make-up free face on its cover, presumably to sell more copies (I wonder if it worked?). These days, Carrie would have been able to sue them for a bit of dosh, especially in litigious USA. But Miranda advises against it (a major error, assuming Carrie might have sued for a small fortune and won). So Carrie has to suck it up, being exposed all over NYC like she's used the worst ageing picture from Faceapp and shared it to a million Instagram followers. Try as I might, I can't sympathise. This is a girl who dresses in 6 inch heels to get milk, for goodness sake. Why turn up to a photoshoot with a lit cigarette and let them test shoot you before they've even given you a coffee? #srsly.

Carrie's bad exposure somehow freaks out all the SATC girls, largely because it's accompanied by a depressing article about single women in their 40s and the horrible lonely lives they lead. (I'm so glad we no longer have to read this sort of outdated mush anymore, and I still can't believe the *New York Magazine* would publish something so tabloid. Aren't they a little above this?)

They immediately all set out to get dates to prove that they are not single and lonely, and don't depend on men (ummm...) and the episode thereafter devotes itself to working out whether "faking it" is sufficient in a relationship. Is it better to fake orgasms than not have any? Is it better to pretend to fall for someone only because they can fix your broken light fitting? Is it better to become fixated on someone you don't even know because they lit your cigarette for you? Well, I'd like to answer those questions for you, but I'm not really sure because we don't get a proper resolution. I think the answer is no. Or maybe yes, for a little while, but then no.

Best Quote: "Hello. You're about a fucking month late." I love this so much I use it where possible.

5 "Four Women and a Funeral"

Carrie goes on a date with Big, but manages not to have sex with him until the end of the episode after she sees him wearing irresistible bowling shoes. All the girls go to a wedding of a famous designer and only Samantha correctly wears the unspoken dress code – the designer's own fashion line. Charlotte meets a widowed man at a nearby gravestone and can't see through his utter falseness in using his dead wife to get women. Samantha's name becomes mud after she is caught with a leg over a married man, by his wife. Miranda buys her own apartment; finally, an SATC girl planning her future!

Ned is a widower, who Charlotte swoons over after meeting him at his wife's grave. He is so fake in showing his heartbreak about his missing wife that he should have been in the last episode. Have you even seen a guy put on such puppy eyes and sob so unconvincingly that you want to choke him? How Charlotte can watch this display and decide he's sensitive and emotional instead of hokey and pathetic I will never know. The girls try to talk her out of this relationship, but he went to Princeton so they have no hope. Eventually, Ned invites all his current shags to meet at his dead wife's graveside for a memorial to her, so Charlotte finds out exactly how many women he is sympathy dating.

Can someone please explain this to me? Would a guy really do that? Don't they usually make a bit of effort to keep their lovers apart from each other? I get that the scene is meant to expose Ned's infidelity, but to be so blatant about it just doesn't meet scrutiny.

Miranda decides to buy an apartment for herself – not with a husband, or boyfriend, but on her very own – and faces a barrage of sexist, irrelevant crap from the people involved in her purchase: the realtor, the mortgage officer, even her future neighbour, who warns her that the previous single owner died in the apartment, alone.

For starters, why would the realtor care who was buying the apartment and whether they were single, engaged, male, female, non-binary or wearing a monkey suit? The realtor still gets their commission, right? Is there any need to repeatedly question Miranda about being a single woman? We are no longer in 1960 where women couldn't get a mortgage in their own names. We are long past this sort of nonsense. We are also past the sort of nonsense where it is standard to have to write your married status on your loan application. These incidents cause Miranda to have a panic attack and wind up in hospital. Shame on you, mortgage officer! And to you too, realtor. Especially you.

Samantha gets sprung making out with some dude she's trying to butter up so she can be on the board of a charity so she can have access to a whole lot of unlisted phone numbers for important people. Shallow. Moving on, Samantha finds herself effectively barred from a stack of hot places around New York because she couldn't control herself with a married man. When will she learn to keep it in her pants?

At the end of the episode, Carrie goes bowling with Big in an attempt to find the most non-sexual activity she can think of so they can stay out of bed, but of course it fails and they end up in bed anyway. Is anyone keeping count, how many times are they back together now?

Best Quote: "I think you made your own bed and you need to lie in it. And you're good at that, aren't you, Samantha?" Shippy Shipman

6 "The Cheating Curve"

The girls explore the notion of cheating, each coming up with a slightly different definition (Samantha's being the most different). Charlotte meets a bunch of Power Lesbians and tries to become one without having sex with a woman. Samantha becomes the first SATC girl to get a pubic hair design. Carrie is back on with Big on the sly and boy are the girls furious once they find out about that. Miranda decides that a man who watches porn while they are having sex is cheating on her.

Charlotte is sick of men (again) and starts to hang out regularly with a bunch of Power Lesbians, although what makes them so powerful I'm not sure. After doing lunch and dancing till dawn with the Lesbians in a nightclub that appears to have a vagina doorway, one of them finally questions Charlotte about her sexual persuasion and Charlotte can't convince them to let her be an Honorary Non-Executive Celibate Power Lesbian and they tell her she can't play with them anymore. Poor Charlotte – she thought she was onto a good thing there. Perhaps there's a group of women somewhere with whom she can have brunch, go shopping, dancing and partying, without being obliged to have sex with them ... oh wait ....

Meanwhile, Miranda starts having sex with a guy who watches porn the whole time they are making sweet sweet love. She quickly grows to hate it, especially when he asks her to shift her head a little to the right so he can fully see the screen. It is a little rude of him, I think. She makes him choose the porn or her, and the porn wins out. I'd be so humiliated! But also I'd feel like I'd dodged a bullet there.

Carrie is sprung by Miranda leaving Big's place early in the morning, walking the streets in her trashy coat and trashier cigarette. She tells Miranda a few lies and changes the subject because she's having sex with Big again and is rightly ashamed of herself. But what I want to know is, what are the chances of Carrie walking along the exact same street that Miranda was on, at the exact same time, especially when Carrie usually hails cabs everywhere? I need a geography lesson on New York because I thought it was a really big crowded place, especially during morning peak hour, and if Carrie was so ashamed she should have been watching where she was going and who she might be likely to bump into.

Carrie later tells the girls that her diaphragm is stuck inside her hoohaa and she is going to have to get one of them to help her to remove it. Ewwwwww!!! This is right up there with Miranda placing Charlotte's vibrator in her purse. Do women like this (who are straight) really exist? I cannot believe Samantha actually went in there and removed someone else's diaphragm. More to the point, I'm not sure why Carrie was having a problem here. I know the diaphragm was a new one, yada yada, but Carrie has worn them plenty of times before. I never had this problem with new contact lenses.

Anyway, the girls take about 35 minutes to realise that if Carrie was wearing a diaphragm then she was having sex with someone, and the whole thing blows up into a big confessional about how she's back with Big and the girls have a go at Carrie and she storms off. Get used to it ladies, because this situation still has a few more seasons to repeat itself.

Samantha finds out that her trainer at the gym, the one she's been having sex with this episode, has shaved not only her but other women's pubic hair into patterns. He probably thought that women didn't parade about the sauna checking each other's muffs out. He'd be wrong, because Samantha and another woman at the gym discover that they have the same lightning bolt pattern carved into their lady fur. Snap!

Best Quote: *"Honey, if you aren't going to eat pussy, then you aren't a dyke". The Chief Power Lesbian, to Charlotte.*

7 "The Chicken Dance"

Miranda accidentally sets up her crush with her interior designer friend and they get engaged and married all in the one episode. Big is probably right when he tells Carrie he gives the marriage three months – why don't we ever find out what happens to the side plot characters? Big acts like a Big prat the entire episode. Samantha remembers she's already fucked a guy – but not until he's halfway through fucking her again. Charlotte, usually mindful that dating is a game and you need to make a man wait for sex for at least 144 dates, has sex with a groomsman she's known for 144 minutes.

Although you gotta feel momentarily sorry for Big, woken by Carrie's middle of the night phone call about some sort of drivel, he goes on to behave appallingly at the wedding: petulantly refusing to sign the wedding card, getting all miffed because his name's on the invitation, taking a phone call while Carrie reads out her awful poem during the speeches, refusing to dance, refusing to stay long enough to watch the cake being cut. So mature. He's just a joy, isn't he? Carrie may be annoying and neurotic, but she knows how to have fun at a party (although there's another hideous dress we could have done without. Who dresses Carrie in these shapeless, skin toned shockers? It smooshes her boobs, makes her look completely washed out and is just a terribly unsophisticated look.) Charlotte, on the other hand, looking a million dollars with her stunning dress and face, lets a cute groomsman have sex with her upstairs *at the wedding on the wedding night bed* - please, Charlotte! Why not follow your own strict policy here – no sex on the first date – and this isn't even a date, it's someone else's wedding where you were paired up with a sleazy tuxedo and his sleazy father. Yet another huge error of judgment and another point the girls should be using with relish next time Charlotte admonishes them for having sex before they really know someone.

Samantha recognises her rerun at the wedding – luckily, or she might have accidentally fucked him a third time.

Miranda, forced to see her crush date her interior designer three or four times and then get engaged at a farewell party she has thrown for him, is feeling very cranky. To add to her indignity, her job at the wedding is to cajole guests to sign the guest book (at which she sucks) and then put the wedding gifts into the car (because this is a job you'd give your friend who's found you a husband). Of all the lousy situations the four SATC girls are in up to their downturned mouths this week, Miranda's wins the saddest sack award. Her third wheel position at the first date of the future betrothed is torture but also quite funny at the same time. She does everything in her power to get between her crush and her designer, but they're not having it. They may as well have told Miranda to just go away already. So she does.

8 "The Man, The Myth, The Viagra"

Carrie continues to try to turn Big into the perfect man or at least pretend he is to her girlfriends. Samantha dates a 72 year old man whose many millions fail to create any sexual attraction to his loose, wrinkly bum. Miranda is humiliated (again! I think this is a trifecta now) by a crappy comedian at a bar when it turns out her date is still married. She then goes on to meet Steve, who pursues in spite of her being generally nasty to him.

Charlotte tries to convince the girls that relationships that were initially bad can come good, and backs up her outlandish statement with anecdotal evidence about a friend of a friend who broke up a marriage and now lives in perfect harmony as her husband's second wife. Charlotte then further attempts to back up her claim by pointing at Carrie, using her on-again off-again relationship with Big as evidence that men can change. Even Carrie looks surprised. Hello, where was Charlotte during the last episode? Oh - that's right, having sex on the wedding bed. Anyway Miranda and Samantha sarcastically scorn the whole concept, but the joke's on them because they immediately go out and find new men, Miranda's (spoiler alert) being the one she eventually marries, so ha ha Miranda! You were wrong.

Firstly, Samantha's new man, Ed. He's first pictured lunching with Donald Trump to give him a bit of street cred (so now Samantha can say she was only two degrees of separation from the President of the USA. Not sure whether that's a good or bad thing). Not only is he lunching with Trump, but he makes it clear that he's investing in Trump and not the other way around, so Samantha is immediately interested, because money. Money money money money. She's not even shy about telling Carrie that the money is what got her over the line, considering he's a bit old for her. Carrie is reasonably disgusted, but she needn't worry. By the time the episode is up, Sam has been given many diamonds, a roll in the hay, gourmet dinners by Ed's ~~slave~~ maid, and a decent glimpse at

Ed's 72 year old arse which is a little…. unappealing. So that's that relationship done.

Steve, on the other hand, is a younger man. He chats up a furious Miranda after she's stood up by Carrie. It really was, by the way, rather appalling of Carrie to leave a message on her dear friend's home phone and then not giving a crap whether the message was received or not. She has a cell phone! And so does Miranda. So I'm with Miranda on this one. She was right to be pissed off, but not necessarily at the bartender. Despite her rudeness to him, he takes her home to her place and tries to get a second date. He's a bit reminiscent of Skipper, Miranda's first puppy-dog man.

Carrie experiences some old-fashioned attention from Big early on, as he sings to her in a restaurant, but his attention giving is short-lived as he refuses to go out in the rain later to meet her friends for dinner. Miranda has a low opinion on Big's lack of showing at dinner, but for some reason Carrie has managed to guilt him enough to make him decide to leave the house (in the rain) and meet up with them all anyway. Miranda is so impressed at Big's effort that she runs outside (in the rain) to apologise to Steve who's just recently copped another big serve of rudeness from her. He didn't get away fast enough – she apologises, and so begins the Steve and Miranda dating merry go round. We shall see what happens.

9 "Old Dogs, New Dicks"

Miranda and Steve have been dating about a minute but it quickly becomes apparent that her long day job and his night shifts are incompatible with daily sex. Carrie discovers yet another flaw in Big: he likes to check out other women while he's with her (doesn't he know that you do that stuff when away from your partner?) In an ultimate show of imitation, one of Samantha's boyfriends has turned into her.

Charlotte is forced to acknowledge an uncircumcised penis, and it's a deal breaker.

In other flaw exposing moments, Big refuses to sleep anywhere but his bed, which means he won't go to Carrie's place. He baulks at giving Carrie a key to his place, letting her wait out the front of his block where she is mistaken for a hooker (we can't really blame the elderly Chinese gentleman for that though, given her appearance). He also sweet talks a waitress into letting him smoke a cigar in a restaurant (I'm so glad oily gits like Big are now prohibited from fouling public air in food establishments). Carrie doesn't deal with any of this in a sensible way, like calmly discussing her grievances with him, or simply refusing to wait in his lobby for him any further. She decides instead to whine about it to the SATC girls.

The main crux of this episode though, is circumcision, and whether circumcised penises are necessary for a relationship (that's a yes from Charlotte) or preferable uncircumcised (yay from Samantha) or neither here nor there (Carrie and Miranda seem to sit on the fence, a mature and rational attitude). What's nonsensical from a statistical point of view though, is that if 85% of males are uncircumcised (*Source: Carrie*) and Samantha has by her admission slept with just 5 uncircumcised men, then she's only had sex with 5.88 men total, which at this point in the series somehow doesn't ring true, does it? The girls don't really buy it either, reminding Samantha that she's slept with more like infinity men. That's a little closer.

Charlotte is being a bit of a twat about all this though. Don't they all look pretty much the same in the semi-dark? Better yet, just don't even look at it. Maybe assess the man on his other qualities (for Charlotte, that's money, looks and money) and then take the relationship from there. Once again I'm a bit disgusted with Charlotte for being so shallow, even going so far as to call it a Shar-Pei. It's like dumping a man because he likes a different china pattern on his crockery than you do, and she's done that, too. Charlotte does get what she deserves though, because after he has a circumcision which she assumes is just for her, he tells her that the real motive was to share his penis with lots of other women. Sometimes Charlotte, you have to be careful what you wish for.

In possibly the most hilarious SATC moment ever, Samantha meets a drag queen she used to fuck who has modelled himself after her, even her name. He looks adorable. I wish someone would be my drag queen.

Miranda is tired of being spooned by Steve and we see several of his attempts to physically hold onto Miranda, including literally getting a leg over, to prevent her from getting out of bed. One day he manages to get her to lie there for 12 hours! She was supposed to be getting her nails done, and her laundry, and a spinning class, but instead he nags her to forget all that and presumably lie and watch him sleep (because he's done night shift). Surely she could have waited for Steve to nod off, then crept away? What a waste of a Saturday.

Carrie eventually has it out with Big, after he accidentally knocks her clear out of bed in the middle of the night and she punches him in the eye in a temper. She tells him exactly what was behind that punch (the women he eyes off, the lack of a key to his apartment, the way he has the upper hand in the relationship and she has to take what she can get). He responds, after a good think about it, that he hates the way she eats oranges in bed (eccchh! Who *does* that?) and she promises not to, so he stays the night in her bed on her sticky orange smelling sheets but also smokes a smelly cigar in her bed, so that evens things up a bit.

10 "The Caste System"

Carrie gets a hideous gift from Big and is taken to an Upper East Side party with Big, where she doesn't fit in at all. Steve can't afford an outrageously expensive suit and won't let Miranda buy it for him because he's threatened by her success (maybe Charlotte was right about something for a change. I'll admit it, but grudgingly, and only once). Charlotte is momentarily blinded by the cuteness of an actor, later finding out what a derp he is. Samantha dates someone with a servant (again) but it all turns to shit.

We just need to have a chat about Charlotte for a minute.

One minute she's making out with a famous actor she just met, in the back of his limo, but she's also berated Carrie for sleeping with someone on a first date. She's lying about her age and getting crabs from a guy 10 years her junior, then she's re-virginising herself before she marries Trey. Sometimes she can't bring herself to drop the F-bomb, instead pausing mid-sentence to allow her friends to fill it in for her, and the next she's swearing left right and centre while giving an opinion on something.

Of all the SATC girls, Charlotte is the one most consistently conflicted. She can't even bring herself to say the word "sex" in front of her mean gay friend Anthony, and has to spell it out, sotto voce. She hates giving blow jobs, but advises Miranda how to talk dirty in bed "c'mon fucker, don't stop". She also tells everyone that Trey licks her arsehole because, well, "we're married".

We come to predict the other personalities: Carrie exhaustingly needy, full of agonising neuroses; Samantha out to try as many penises as she can in this lifetime; and Miranda always ready to pour cold water on everything. At least you know what you're getting with those three. But with Charlotte, it's Laura Ashley one minute and Roseanne Barr the next. Who are you, Charlotte?

Ok, that's over.

Moving on, Miranda wants to take Steve to a fancy lawyer work party thing but is repulsed by his only suit, a gold corduroy number which would actually look really cool and hipster in 2019. Steve can't bring himself to allow Miranda to buy him a brand new suit, dismissing her pleading to let her do so. He scrapes his entire life savings together plus a bit of credit and buys the suit to protect his pride, even though the cost breaks him into a cold sweat. Later, he blows the pride and returns the suit. He turns up at Miranda's in casualwear and dumps her, for being successful, as she puts it. Again I am relieved to note that 20 years later, this would be a non-issue. Men these days earn less than women quite often, and today's generation of 30 somethings have no issue accepting something for nothing (just look at all the 30 somethings who haven't even moved out of their parents' home yet).

My question is: that suit was already altered to fit him. How did he talk the shop into accepting it back?

Charlotte follows her cute airheaded actor and his entourage around for a bit, all giggly and gooey eyed about her new groupie status. But it ends abruptly when he asks her to go into the bathroom, stick her finger up her hoohaa and bring it back to him so he can smell it. Isn't that the grossest thing ever? Reminds me never to date a famous young actor. Although the chances of that were pretty slim to be honest.

Carrie is taken to a snobby party by Big, carrying a hideous purse he has given her. At the party, we see similar purses carried by all the hoity toity women in attendance. It's a hard shell of a thing in the shape of a duck and looks to be impractical as well as difficult to hold, but the moment of receiving a gift, any gift from Big, causes Carrie to blurt out the unthinkable: That she loves Big. Big doesn't return the sentiment so now everything's awkward.

They covered this one in Seinfeld too, when George declares it to his woman of the episode and she too doesn't return the sentiment. Both Carrie and George now face the difficult situation of being the one to put it out there first when they weren't sure of a return, and they both go on to suffer a tenuous grip on the relationship. In Carrie's case it ends in a fight with Big that very night. She goes home with the waiter, who quits his job that he probably needs without giving the slightest shit, after getting caught showing Carrie his pubic tattoo when he should have been carrying platters.

They hit Carrie's sack and they are woken the next morning by Big's phone call to respond to Carrie's blurt with a blurt of his own: that he fucking loves her, ok? He really is a dick though. What a way to tell that to someone that you allegedly love. I don't buy it. In any case, Carrie is relieved to find out that she doesn't have to feel guilty about the waiter because the waiter confirms that they didn't do anything (was she really so drunk that she can't remember? How old is this woman again?)

Boy, a lot goes on in this episode, doesn't it? We haven't even covered Samantha yet. I'll be brief: Sam's new wealthy man has a servant who decides to get rid of Sam by being completely two faced and turning her employer against Sam. It works a treat and Sam is ousted from the bed and the apartment. The end.

11 "Evolution"

Since Miranda is no longer having regular sex, she decides to go off the pill (but Miranda, there's always next episode). Charlotte dates a gay straight man. We meet an ex of Samantha's who she had actually fallen in love with – and those kind of exes are thin on the ground for Samantha. Carrie tries to leave some of her girly stuff at Big's but he's not having that clutter in his bathroom cabinet.

Miranda finds out that one of her ovaries has stopped producing eggs. How do they test for that exactly? Wouldn't you need some kind of specialised investigation to discover such a thing? It's not as though Miranda was trying to get knocked up and having trouble getting there.

She had no reason to be questioning her ovaries about their egg production and whether they're just shooting blanks.

Somehow, Charlotte finds herself on a non-date with a pastry chef she thinks is gay, until he plants a sloppy kiss on her to say goodnight. Confused, she takes Carrie and Stanford (there should be more of Stanford) to meet him and assess whether Stephan is a gay man in the closet, or a straight man who has been so exposed to hair dye, gym memberships and café lattes that he's halfway to being gay. These days, they have a new word for that – non-binary – but back in the 90s it was a confusing time where it was rude to assume and rude to ask. Stanford assures Charlotte that her pastry chef is straight, because if you're gay you KNOW you're gay. So why did he have to meet the guy to ascertain that?

Later, after some amazing sex, Charlotte is relieved to affirm that he is straight, but then disappointed when Stephan goes all girly and screams over a mouse caught on sticky paper in his kitchen. It's a deal breaker: Charlotte doesn't want to have to catch mice, so we'll add that to the list of reasons why Charlotte won't date a man. Afraid of mice. Tick.

Samantha decides to be a big tease to a guy she once loved – the only guy she's ever loved and who's ever hurt her – by going on a date with him but not consummating it. Her big plan is to be completely gorgeous, make him want her and then metaphorically slap him in the face. These ideas are only good if you know you can go through with it.

She blows her game plan by falling for him all over again after having sex with him, then is enraged when he announces that it was just a fuck and he's going back to his wife. Why couldn't you play it cool, Samantha? Why did you have to throw a tanty and tell him what you had planned to do and how he's ruined it all? So much more mature to act like you don't care. Cry about it later if you must, but as a mistress of game playing it bemuses me how badly you lost that one, Sam.

Carrie tries to leave half a drugstore of stuff at Big's, but it backfires (this is, after all, the same guy who won't give her a key to his apartment and tells her he loves her using the F word in the middle of the sentiment). I also wish Carrie would have played it cool here. She should have taken Charlotte's advice and not tried to encroach upon Big's territory, because he's cold and has boundaries that are not going to be cracked by sheer force, ie. by leaving a hairdryer in his bathroom cabinet. Big delivers all her stuff back to Carrie in an expensive shopping bag, momentarily making her think it was a gift. Boom! Even Big has the grace to look a bit embarrassed about being so petty. He ends up giving her space for one pair of panties. But the win is short-lived (see next episode).

Best Quote: Stephan: "If I were gay, I'd be gay". Well said.

12 "La Douleur Exquise!"

Big is sentenced to several months in Paris due to a big-ass deal for work, and Carrie takes it very personally, making it all about her. Miranda is caught having sex with her man, by his parents. Samantha finally gets the client of her dreams: an S&M club opening. Charlotte gets some free shoes.

Carrie's relationship with Big comes to an abrupt end again after he tells her he might need to stay in Paris a while for his job. She is furious that she isn't a "factor" in his decision making, and wakes him at 5:30am before an important client meeting with a nonsensical drunken call to his Paris hotel room (I don't know how she got the number, because I'm pretty sure Big wouldn't have given it out). This is Carrie at her worst: she is acting like she expected him to quit his job for her. The SATC girls try to cheer her up a bit, but Carrie loudly fusses about it before deciding that the best course of action would be for her to go to Paris with him if phone sex isn't enough. Big tries to hide his horror, and offers her a very unconvincing reassurance that he loves her (he can barely spit the words out) but it's the end of another Big/Carrie era and she lets him fly away, which is what you should always do when it's fairly apparent that someone just isn't that into you.

We are treated to another hilarious appearance from Stanford as he sheepishly explains to Carrie that he's been online on a gay website posing as Rick9plus, chatting up someone called BigTool4U. Stanford is nervous that in a proposed meeting with BigTool4U, he might be intimidated by BigTool4U's incredible buff physique. Carrie reminds him that his own username might be a slight exaggeration, and Stanford concedes that "I am so getting your point". He agrees to meet his internet lover in real life at a gay bar, and when he arrives is forced to strip to his underwear to get entrance. What??? That cannot be real. Not only does he comply, but we never get to meet BigTool4U – Stanford meets someone else instead. So really, you don't need to set up a profile on a dating site when you're gay. You can just go to a gay bar.

Charlotte visits a shoe store and is given a pair of free shoes in exchange for allowing the salesman to give her a foot rub. Fantastic, I say! What's wrong with that? But Miranda and Carrie see differently, for some reason (like they've never accepted a freebie) and shame Charlotte into going back to return the shoes (even though they've been worn). Instead of returning them, Charlotte ends up being a foot model for the salesman so he can slip all the new shoes onto her feet and get off on it (and pray that no one else walks in on this beautiful moment). Charlotte doesn't speak of it to the girls though, she knows they'll just think it's icky. Whatever. Free shoes, yeah.

In a rare instance, Samantha doesn't have sex with anyone in this episode.

As for Miranda, she's having sex all over the city in strange places, like a 16-year-old with no other choice. Her man's fetish is getting off in public. It was all going well until he lets his parents walk in on them doing it. You can tell he planned that, and it's a fairly big red flag – public sex is fine, but involving your parents is a whole new level of eeeeyechhhh. Lucky for us, it's a deal-breaker for Miranda and she's outta there.

13 "Games People Play"

Carrie translates her hurt over Big into a never-ending series of rants about how great she is and how much she pities Big for not choosing her over his stupid career. We see Miranda's boob for the first time. Samantha tries to turn her latest man's enthusiasm for sports into enthusiasm for fucking her, but sadly fails. Charlotte doesn't get up to anything much.

Carrie's friends can no longer handle her endless carrie-ing on (see what I did there) about Big, which is starting to sound inane (Carrie even refers to herself as the "poof" in the relationship). Wanting to make it stop, the SATC girls send her to the "It" therapist Dr G., who figures Carrie out in 4 minutes flat: she picks the wrong men. (It's probably a common diagnosis for Dr G's patients). Not learning her lesson at all, Carrie immediately picks up Jon Bon Jovi (aaaack!) in her therapist's waiting room no less, and sleeps with him before even finding out why he needs therapy. Another mistake there Carrie, but it does lead to an amazing epiphany: she finally realises that she picks the wrong men. I think even the viewers could have told her that. In her loving post-coital discussion with Jon where he says he loses interest in women after sex, she responds with how she picks the wrong men. Hey, at least there was total honesty.

Miranda sees a hot guy through her apartment window and he flashes her his bum. She responds by flashing him her boob. If this were 20 years later, we'd all be like *yawn* because that's pretty tame stuff given the advent of social media and #dicpic, #boob, #lenadunham and #nude. But at the time, it's pretty racy (#hardtobelieve). It does unfortunately end sadly for Miranda though, because she finds out after meeting the guy in a supermarket that he's gay and couldn't care less if he saw a naked boob. At least he wouldn't be interested in taking a pic with his iPhone and posting it on Facebook, though, so she's safe there.

After a heavy discussion about game playing with men, the girls head to a sports bar (*why*, of all places?) where they are mostly ignored by a bunch of men watching sport loudly with all their testosterone on display. Samantha still manages to get picked up though, by Don the Knicks fan. She goes home with him of course and is an immediate Knicks convert, meaning that if the Knicks win she gets happy sex from Don and if they don't win she gets nada. We are forced to endure watching Samantha screaming fuck at the basketball players on the TV screen in the misguided hope that this will help them win, and when they finally do and the season is over Don merrily transfers his attention to baseball instead and she knows it's time to quit sports.

*Special Note: Jon Bon Jovi. How **hot** is he here?*

Best Quote: "This is Manhattan. Even the shrinks have shrinks." – Stanford. How I love him.

14 "The Fuck Buddy"

Carrie turns to her fuck buddy to extract a relationship out of him. Miranda dates a sarcastic, negative, rude lawyer and even though they are a lot alike, she can't stand him. Charlotte decides to date as many men as she can, in order to increase her chances at the elusive

marriage target. Samantha gets herself off eavesdropping on the creepy couple having sex next door.

Although to be fair, Samantha didn't know they were creepy until she actually met them. She's annoyed about the loud sex, but not because it's keeping her awake – this is Samantha we're talking about here – she's annoyed because they've selfishly left her out of proceedings, so she uses the opportunity to loudly masturbate to make sure they can hear her.

There's so much that's gross about this I'm not sure where to start. We've already covered threesomes, do we have to go there again? Apparently yes, because Samantha knocks on their door wearing something tarty and scanty (because that's a safe, normal thing to do to your neighbours who you've never met) in the hope of joining in. It's a low point in Samantha's desperation. She discovers that they're not really "her type" (not even close) and will now have to face them probably every single day until one of them moves, after they've all heard each other having sex or masturbating and also seen wearing their sexywear. It's too much.

Carrie calls up her fuck buddy (and can you believe the girls have to explain to Charlotte what a fuck buddy is? Come ON. It's season 2 already) and has sex with him. There is absolutely zero chemistry between them – the awkwardness of the conversation that follows the sex is cringeworthy, even as a viewer – but Carrie nevertheless decides to ask him out for dinner. He assumes she meant more sex, but she really meant dinner (he's a bit disappointed). And they go to a very uncomfortable meal where he displays a complete lack of sense of humour, an inability to converse about much else than his (boring) job and unwillingness to taste the sushi. Thank goodness Carrie decides to write him off forever (after one more go in the sack). Bye-bye, John.

Charlotte takes the awful advice of her friends and arranges two dates in one night, even though there was no real reason to do that. Last time I checked, there were 7 days and 7 nights in a week and the weeks don't seem to be in any danger of ending in the near future, so why the panic?

However, she doesn't think ahead enough to plan a credible exit from the first date so she can make the second. Have you ever seen a sore throat appear so suddenly and implausibly? It's amazing her date fell for it. She should have warned him at the beginning that she was feeling a little unwell and couldn't stay out too late. Plan wisely next time, Charlotte.

Her first date, who she's known only two hours, brings chicken soup to her apartment, as she's finishing off her second date right outside it. Wow! Bad timing. It's a shame she pissed Man #1 off by letting him catch her with Man #2; Man #1 seems like the nicest guy in the whole of SATC. His swift exit, catching a cab with Man #2 into the night together, is hilarious and quite deserved.

15 "Shortcomings"

We finally meet a family member of the York family: Charlotte's brother Wesley, married to Lesley but about to divorce. They must have been sick of all the giggling. Carrie falls in love with her new boyfriend's family, and finds breaking up with them harder than breaking up with her boyfriend. Miranda meets a man at the gym during children's hour and finds that he is the father of one of the little turds. Samantha has sex with Wesley and Charlotte is displeased.

Carrie is invited to speak at a seminar by her new boyfriend's dad (see season 3, episode 16 to understand why it was a good thing she never took him up on it). Carrie's boyfriend's mum, on the other hand, tells Carrie she should write about revirginization in one of her columns. It makes me wonder if either of them have actually read the column. It's not about virgins in any way, and a writer doesn't necessarily make a speaker. Moving on to the boyfriend himself, he has a terrible problem: premature ejaculation. And by premature, I mean before it even gets out of his pants. There might have been a solution for this: wait 20 minutes and try again? But no one thinks of this so Carrie bravely raises the issue with him, and he is offended and refuses to discuss it. (Selfish.) Seems another girlfriend has discussed it, though – not with him but with his mother. (Awkward.) Carrie wants to remain friends with the family but when you've already discussed your boyfriend's sexual issues with them it's pretty much over.

Miranda's gym has a family hour – which means that when adults are trying to get a serious workout done, children are running all over the gym, bouncing on the equipment, yelling and being general menaces. This must break quite a number of health and safety regulations. It could be quite dangerous if, for example, a small child was hit by someone performing deadlifts, or someone were to trip over a child running across their path, falling onto a moving treadmill and sustaining head injuries. Just a couple of scenarios that come to mind.

Anyhow, the worst thing that happens to Miranda is that some kid presses all the buttons in the lift, thus making her late for something, and the father of the kid asks Miranda out as kind of an apology. Miranda's worry is that she won't like the kid, and the worrying was not in vain. He's not a very nice kid, and his father overreacts a little when Miranda accidentally slams a door in his face, banning Miranda from the house henceforth. It was an accident, dude! And the kid, what a drama queen.

Samantha and Charlotte have their first fight, over Samantha's seduction of her brother Wesley. Charlotte wakes to find Samantha in her house, rifling through her coffee pods in just a t-shirt. Wesley has enjoyed a night with Samantha as he has had no sex for two years and is getting divorced.

I agree that it is definitely icky to find Samantha half dressed in your kitchen first thing in the morning, but we are all adults here, are we not? Surely it's not Charlotte's business in any way to approve of who Wesley wants to fuck. Accusing Samantha of being a slut was not the best way to handle it, even if there is a hint of truth in it. At least Charlotte was big enough to apologise, and with muffins too.

16 "Was It Good For You?"

In this episode, we cover off alcoholism, voyeurism, more threesomes, gays, self-esteem, and going tantric. There's a lot going on.

Let's start with Charlotte and Samantha, who both receive rude shocks to their confidence after Charlotte's man falls asleep on her during sex and Samantha is seduced and then dumped by two gay men. In both cases, there is no need to be insulted: Charlotte's man is a very busy doctor who's just done a long day at the surgery, and Samantha's men were, and this is crucial, *gay*. (They also look like twin brothers, but we won't go there). Anyone with any faith in themselves would have brushed these experiences aside and moved on, but it's SATC so Charlotte is devastated and decides she needs sex lessons - and she expects all her friends to enrol with her. Sure, why not, they say.

So off they troop to a private apartment and line up on a couch where they watch a naked man being given tantric sex by his wife. I'm not sure what tantric sex is, but here it doesn't look too dissimilar to giving a guy a hand job. There's not really enough of a visual to make a judgement call. Anyway, the girls can't help themselves and crack jokes and generally show disrespect except for Charlotte who tells them all to grow up and behave themselves. (It is bloody funny though, especially when Miranda says

"Perineum: Latin for 'not without an engagement ring.' ")

Miranda is then punished for her lack of decorum by being sprayed with jizz – it lands on her nose and hair – and not even noticing it's there while the girls cack themselves laughing. This is some magic tantric spunk to travel that far across a room.

Meanwhile, Carrie has picked up a recovering alcoholic after he throws a lit cigarette butt at her arm by accident. (That would be a deal breaker for me. Smoking and littering too! Hard pass). Carrie refuses to take his situation seriously by acting thusly:

- Telling him she adores alcoholics and hopes to be one
- Helping him blow his twelve month commitment to the AA program when he's almost completed it
- Becoming offended when he tries to date her a few times before they have sex
- Being flattered that he's transferred his addiction directly to her

It all blows up in her face when he gets horribly drunk after she tells him to back off. He strips naked in the street while singing loudly and smashing bottles outside her apartment, and Carrie is horrified but also continues to wonder if she was so good in bed that she was the cause of his relapse. Er, I very much doubt that.

17 "Twenty-Something Girls vs. Thirty-Something Women"

Charlotte starts talking and acting like a 20-something in order to fool her latest man, a 26-year-old who parties every year at the Hamptons. Miranda is offended by the presence of all the 20-somethings at the

Hamptons. *Samantha's client list gets stolen by her ditsy employee who uses it to throw a party at the Hamptons. And worst of all for Carrie, this is where we meet Natasha – at the Hamptons.*

Charlotte begins a summer beach fling with a much younger man, who thinks she's 27 and later accuses her of lying to him about her age. "You deceived me" he whines, as though she sold him a fake Rolex. Charlotte rebuts by telling him that he made the assumption, she just didn't correct him.

But ahhh, let's go back a few scenes where Charlotte firmly tells Miranda that she's 27, in full hearing of the man she's lying on top of. You may not have told him directly, Charlotte, but what you did do was kind of the same thing, hey.

Most amusing of all is the fact that Charlotte gets crabs from the guy, and the person to diagnose her is the 20-something virgin Laurel who's been hanging round Carrie like a limpet for the past couple of days. It's great that a virgin has the knowledge of these things without having to experience them. She suddenly seems like the smartest person in the house.

And just onto Laurel: here is a straight-laced girl who is cheerily saving herself for marriage, but is also a huge fan of Carrie's column which is full of stuff about men and sex. I have absolutely no idea why Laurel would be so enamoured of Carrie and why she wants Carrie, of all the writers in NY, to be a mentor to her as she embarks upon her writing career. Why does an intentional virgin worship a sex columnist who writes for a low-grade newspaper?

As you've figured by now, this episode takes place at the Hamptons. There is a big party that Samantha is invited to by Nina, the assistant she fired who stole her Rolodex client list. Samantha really should have included a clause in Nina's contract forbidding her to steal company information upon termination of employment, and it's a shame Miranda didn't think to advise her of this for next time. Anyway, in a strategic move that is beyond excellent, Samantha makes the best effort at payback that could have ever been devised: she introduces Charlotte's crab man to Nina, thus ensuring that Nina will almost certainly get crabs. It's the cleverest thing she's ever done.

But enough of all that. The episode's big twist is that Carrie stumbles upon Big and his new girlfriend, who are coincidentally attending the very same shindig that the SATC girls are at. Natasha is everything Carrie is not: tall, brunette, 26 or 27, impossibly pretty, and seemingly very mature and confident, given the way she reacts when she meets Carrie. Graciously, she smiles and says 'I've heard so much about you!" which is probably a lie, so she's charming too. Then she quickly excuses herself from a situation that she senses is about to get very awkward. So she's also got good people skills. It's no wonder Carrie runs away to blow chunks on the beach after she discovers Big's betrayal. I know they were on a break, but still. Even Big admits it wasn't the way he had planned for her to find out. (I can't help but wonder: when did he intend to break it to her? I'm guessing never). All I can caution you is that it's about to get even worse, so don't be going on any rollercoasters, Carrie.

18 "Ex and the City"

Carrie lives through all of our worst nightmares: she discovers that the love of her life is engaged. Miranda tries to be friends with Steve after snubbing him in the street. Samantha tries to have sex with a man who possesses an impossibly large penis. Charlotte is boring about horses.

Although Big wishes he could have broken the news about his recent engagement in other ways, the fact is that any which way, Carrie would have gone beserk and lost her shit, so he needn't feel too upset about it. At least the news was direct from him, and it was open and timely (before it made the newspapers). Inviting her to the actual engagement might have taken things a touch too far, though.

Miranda sees Steve in the street, and instead of greeting him cheerfully and behaving like a grown up, she panics, grabs Carrie and flees, in full view of Steve. I can't remember the details of their break-up – let me just check.

Oh yeah, that's right. He broke up with her because she earns a lot more than him and he felt embarrassed about his gold cord suit and his general poverty. But that's no reason to panic and run, is it? Miranda – and I've said this before – is a lawyer. Although I'm not sure what kind of law she actually practices, she must deal with confrontation, difficult people and situations all the live long day, 60 hours a week. Why can't she just put her game bitch face on and act like she doesn't give a toss? That's what I'd do. Running away from someone just makes them think you like them.

To follow-up, Steve does a drop-in on Miranda at her apartment to call her shitty for her behaviour, and then admits he's being kind of shitty, randomly turning up to tell her that. It all ends in bed, of course. Steve is now officially a fuck buddy. Boom!

So: the big plot line in this episode is that Carrie finds out Big is serious about his new girl – so serious in fact, that he's proposed to her within a matter of months. We've all been here - or in a similar situation – where the love of your life hurts you big time. So while I agree that it's pure hell and the moment can catch you by surprise, the best way to act is nonchalant. Grit your teeth, wish him well and let it all out when you get home. Easier said than done, I know. But try not to knock over chairs and fall down a staircase as you make a grand exit after expressing all your hysterical sentiments. It's not cool. Better yet: practice avoidance, which is what Carrie should have done. The girls spent a while chatting about whether you can be friends with an ex and whether it's a good idea, but no one thought to mention the obvious: if you aren't *over* him, then you aren't *ready*. And that day might never come, so don't consider calling him up for lunch until it does.

Charlotte has flashbacks to where she was thrown from a horse many years ago. She decides to be brave and rides a horse again. I fail to see the point of all this.

Samantha is picked up on the street by a cocky man who rightly guesses that she'd be pretty easy to get into bed. But he has a challenge for her: the biggest cock in the world, apparently. Bless Sam; she gives it a couple of really good goes before she concedes defeat and asks him if they could just be friends because her hoohaa can't accommodate him. If Samantha can't handle him, I wonder who could?

The episode and season ends with three of the SATC girls singly (badly) "The Way We Were". It's so awful and it goes on way too long (I think Samantha would agree with me there) although for some reason it does get Samantha all sentimental and she tearfully blurts that she misses James, of all people. The one with the gherkin penis. How she manages to link her frustrating relationship with him to a badly rendered Way We Were is random.

Quote: "Women are for friendship, men are for fucking." – Samantha, of course. She still hasn't learned anything after two seasons.

10 Dumb Charlotte Philosophies

1. You only get one great love
2. Women shouldn't own their own apartments; they should rent so they aren't a threat to men
3. It's so cute when a cute guy publicly urinates against a wall
4. You can't have a relationship with a man who has a different household crockery design aesthetic than yourself
5. You should never do a number two at a man's place
6. If you don't have sex for a long time, you can re-virginise yourself
7. It takes half the length of time you went out with someone to get over them
8. When you get married, you get a whole week of your own for everyone to focus on just you
9. Men don't marry up-the-butt girls
10. Uncircumcised penises are not acceptable

Season 3

1 "Where There's Smoke..."

Carrie starts dating a politician who seems (correct me if I'm wrong) to be over her dating age limit, previously self-prescribed as 50. Samantha has sex with a hot fireman who has absolutely nothing between the ears. Miranda gets her eyes lasered. Charlotte is sick of waiting for the right man and gets horribly drunk and hungover.

Well; if you ever needed confirmation that Samantha needs no intellect, sense of humour, warmth, mental connection, mutual hobbies or any personality at all in a man she's looking to lay, this episode will give it to you. I'm surprised she doesn't just buy a blow-up doll already, because chances are it would satisfy her just as much.

Nevertheless, Samantha meets a fireman at a fireman-catwalk-calendar-audition thingy (is that an adequate description?) all the way out at Staten island and goes home with him, even though he seems to have issues with basic comprehension and vocabulary. She meets him again at his fire station (yes, his place of *work, while he is at work*) and after realising that it's not exactly the fantasy she had in mind, decides to fuck her dull fireman anyway right up against his fire truck, then step into some other guy's uniform and parade around in it a bit. Samantha, what if there was a fire? Oh wait – there is a fire!

I'm pretty sure that hosting an unauthorised visitor in your fire station is against terms of employment for any fireman, not to mention fucking them on duty while leaning on your fire safety machinery. But the worst that happens is that Sam gets sprung almost naked by the entire fire squad as well as some horrified passers-by. Will she ever learn?

Speaking of learning, Carrie buys yet another pair of Jimmy Choo shoes. She is then pursued by a persistent politician who continues to show an interest even after Carrie tells him she has never voted in a New York election and really only has one hobby – shopping. So how did she meet this guy? He's a fellow judge on a panel at the fireman-catwalk-calendar-audition thingy. I'm not sure why a male would be invited to judge this sort of competition unless he was gay – not trying to be sexist or anything but why select a silver haired, straight, local politician? Is it good for his local profile? In any case Carrie resists the idea of a date because she's too scarred from her Big breakup, but before long they're making out in a cloakroom and boom! he's Carrie's rebound guy. It seems doomed from the start, doesn't it.

At the very same place where Carrie and Samantha meet their latest shags, Charlotte gets disgustingly drunk and decides that this will be the year she gets married. Amazingly, wishing for something will actually work for her, sort of. Note: thankfully, it won't be the floppy haired bully she meets in this episode. Stay tuned.

Steve seems to have changed his mind about Miranda. When they broke up it was because he was too belittled by her wealth to be seen in the same room as her, but Steve now seems to have got past that and is hanging around, offering sex on tap and to be Miranda's aide after she has laser eye surgery.

Miranda has grudgingly agreed, on her doctor's insistence, to bring a friend to help her home and to bed for the recovery. She has chosen Carrie and firmly told Steve not to bother, after he has practically begged her to let him help. But Carrie cancels at the last minute – she's such a reliable friend, isn't she. Steve magically appears, summoned by Carrie – well, at least she arranged a replacement so she's not a total ditz – and is Miranda grateful? Not exactly. She snaps at Steve and as usual he puts up with it, making sure she is safely in bed with her eye goggles on. When she wakes up the next morning, the laser seems to have fixed more than her eyes, as she lovingly gazes at Steve and hopefully decides to be nicer to him. It's a miracle!

2 "Politically Erect"

Here we cover off golden showers and who's into them (can you guess?) Steve tells Miranda he loves her and she decides to let him keep seeing her as there's no one else on her radar anyway. Charlotte throws a Used Date party. Samantha has sex with a horny munchkin.

Let's talk about Samantha's little man.

For some reason, Samantha can't bear the thought of a man being significantly shorter than her, for reasons which aren't explained. After all, she's attracted to him enough to have sex with him – and he's good looking, he dresses well, he's quite witty. He's got a lot more going for him than that dumb-arse fireman from last episode. Hasn't she heard of Nicole Kidman and Tom Cruise? All right, maybe that's not the best example.

But how short *is* he? Well, that varies. In one scene, his nose fits perfectly between her breasts when they are standing facing each other, so he's more than a full head shorter. In a later scene, the top of his head reaches her earlobe, and that's while she's wearing heels.

What I don't understand is why they couldn't get a really short guy, instead of having Samantha stand on a box for half of the scenes. It's comical when he blows a raspberry into her chest, followed by Samantha's rolled eyes. Heh. But it all turns to bullshit when it appears he's not really *that* short.

Charlotte meets a happily engaged couple who met at a party where you bring someone you're interested in so you can "swap" them out for someone else. Although it's the greatest idea Charlotte has ever heard, I foresee a few issues. Half the people at the party think they're with someone who likes them, but are very likely to find out they are there to be dumped.

It's surprising that the only person who discovers this minor detail is Samantha's little man. Everyone else seems too stupid to understand what's going on. It's a social minefield, full of opportunities for horrible things to happen once people realise they're being publicly rejected. The only way it could work safely is if everyone was clued up to the actual purpose of the gathering and know they are there to be traded. Which brings me to another couple of points: how did Charlotte know so many people who could bring someone they weren't interested in? I'd be embarrassed to even ask my friends to attend a party like this. It's like a swinger party, but without the sex. What do you put on the invitation? Do you even send invitations? Or is it all done by stealth? They didn't have private Facebook events for this sort of thing in the 90s.

Meh. Maybe I'm just overthinking all this.

Meanwhile, Carrie seems to be getting along with her over-50 rebound guy. Until he asks her to participate in a golden shower with him. Samantha is full of her usual good advice to just go along with it (there's nothing she would advise against, let's face it) but Carrie is unable to face the thought of it. Instead of just politely saying it's not really her thing but thanks for the offer, she nearly chokes herself eating spicy food without water during her dinner date so she won't have to pee. The logic of this is…. well, there's no logic to this really. You probably should be in a shower situation to give or get a golden shower, I'm just guessing, and that's not likely to happen during dinner. It is a relief when Carrie does finally explain that she's just not into it. Simples, Carrie.

Side Note: Why does Carrie always drag the whole top sheet off the bed with her when she leaves the bed and goes into the bathroom? Hasn't she got a robe?

3 "Attack of the 5'10" Woman"

Sigh. Another silly plotline for Charlotte, who tiptoes ditzily around the spa changerooms with pursed lips and a towel around her armpits because she's too shy to walk about naked, then complains about her massive thighs throughout the episode. Samantha gets wind of a special deal at her beautician's but it backfires on her. Miranda hires a maid. Carrie finds she is sharing a changeroom with her nemesis, Big's stunning model wife.

Charlotte has a hard time walking around the changerooms and spa topless, because she's shy. Refer to season 1, episode 5, where she lets an artist create an eight foot painting of her cunt. Also refer to season 5 episode 1 where Charlotte flashes a boob to a sailor in a nightclub. #paradoxical.

Anyway, why make a big deal about all this? If you aren't comfortable walking about naked, then you really don't have to. There's no need to whine to your friends that you didn't grow up in a "naked house", whatever that is. Just keep your towel on, Charlotte, and do us all a favour. No one cares.

Samantha puts her foot in it, or more accurately, her hand on it, when she gropes a male masseur. She's heard on the grapevine that he likes to go down on his female clients after he's massaged them (for some reason they are all OK with this). Samantha wants in on it (of course she does) and takes matters (his penis) into her own hands when it appears he's not making the same moves on her after the frontal massage is over. Samantha: maybe you just aren't his type. Ever heard of letting a guy make a move? If he doesn't, play it cool and walk away. It's lucky the #meetoo movement hadn't gotten up and running in the 90s because this would be waved about as an example of extreme sexual harassment and everyone would have been publicly shamed: the masseur, the clients, the salon and Samantha. As a result of all this seedy behaviour, there is a job lost, employers upset and Samantha is ticked off by her angry fellow ex-clients at the salon. #deserved.

I'm not sure why Miranda needs a maid – maybe she's really messy – but Magda is religious and judgy, so it's the ultimate indignity when she opens Miranda's top dresser drawer and finds her vibrator. Who opens someone's drawer in front of them? Magda really should have done that when she had the place to herself, if she's really that snoopy, and she definitely should not have followed up by replacing said vibrator with the Virgin Mary. Since Miranda is someone who can't stand a man showering after sex and declares Catholics deal-breakers, it's surprising that Magda goes on to stay with Miranda for many years, eventually becoming her nanny as well as her cleaner. I kind of expected her to be out the door after she'd God-blessed Miranda for being unsure about whether she ever wants to get married.

Carrie bumps into Natasha, Big's impossibly beautiful wife, in a changeroom while Carrie is in her underwear. Carrie is embarrassed again, as she always seems under-dressed when Natasha is around (recall the cowgirl boob tube ensemble at the Hamptons). Natasha is as usual gracious and polite. They discover they are attending the same function, a women in the arts lunch thingy, so Carrie decides to impress Natasha with a new dress that costs a month's rent, and new heels. At least Carrie admits she has a Natasha-specific obsession, but again she has proved that her neuroses have obliterated any rational thought processes. It was 100% certain that Carrie would have already possessed a nice frock and matching shoes in her wardrobe that Natasha would not have seen before. Sometimes I wish Carrie's friends would stop her throwing her limited cash on totally unnecessary fashion items. Then she may not have wound up with (spoiler alert) $40,000 of shoes and "nowhere to live".

Unfortunately it was doubly a terrible waste of money for Carrie, who spends all that dosh impressing no one as Natasha is a no show at the event. Samantha is at her rudest, calling Natasha a bitch for being sick, referring to all the women in the arts attendees as "bitches who need to be put in their places", talking loudly about how she deserved to be eaten out by the masseur, and lastly, finding someone who used to know Natasha who has a fairly boring couple of things to say about the skeletons in Natasha's closet. None of this makes Carrie feel any better, and if I were Carrie I'd probably not be taking Samantha to any classy events in the future, either.

Ironic Plot Point: the SATC girls being very disparaging about women who marry and give up their careers, which is apparently what Charlotte secretly dreams about, as it's what she eventually does.

Inexplicable Quote: Carrie telling Miranda that "It's a good thing she got married. The woman's an idiot!" after receiving a thank you card from Natasha with a grammatical error on it. I can't help but wonder: what does getting married have to do with not being able to tell the difference between "their" and "there"?

4 "Boy, Girl, Boy, Girl..."

We return to a world of 20 somethings, as Carrie dates one and Samantha hires one to work for her. Charlotte lets a photographer dress her as a man and photograph her. Miranda agrees to let Steve move into her apartment.

It's supposed to be another SATC ground-breaking moment; an actual woman-to-woman kiss, which in the 90s wasn't really shown very much and certainly not on mainstream television. But all I can think about when Alanis Morissette tongue-kisses Carrie is *but Carrie literally just blew out cigarette smoke two seconds ago!* Eyagh. There was no beauty in that for me.

The kiss happens at a party that Carrie's 20 something guy, Sean, takes her to. Sean has openly told Carrie that he is bisexual and Carrie pretends to be all cool with it but inwardly she is not coping at all. She can't stop asking him questions about his past relationships, asking him to rank her against his female and male exes. Just because someone is bi doesn't mean they should have to answer neurotic questions from their current partner about how well they kiss compared to everyone else. It's so very high school. And so is walking out of the party without saying goodbye to Sean, and never seeing him again despite him seeming to be quite a nice guy.

Samantha hires an arrogant arsehole to work for her (she seems to have no knack for employing good staff, as this is a situation she found herself with Nina back in episode 17, last season). However, there is a whole list of qualities Samantha doesn't look for in a man, as we've previously discussed, and we can now add "a good work ethic" and "manners" to that list. She fires her arrogant assistant but it's great because that means she can now fuck him (although I'm not sure why she had to wait until she'd fired him, given what we know about her personal values).

Charlotte holds a gallery exhibition for a dude who cross-dresses his subjects and photographs them. He appears to have a bit of a thing for Charlotte, asking her to be his subject for a photo shoot. Charlotte complains that she's too much of a girly-girl but he manages to talk her into it anyway. Somehow they end up having sex as well as getting a picture taken, but Charlotte is so embarrassed by her "forwardness" that she can't see him again. I don't get why Charlotte would be embarrassed about this. It's not the first nor will it be the last time she grabs a guy and kisses him. He didn't even seem to mind, at all. In a future episode she'll be asking Trey to marry her, and if that's not forward then I don't know what is.

Steve is bugging Miranda by taking up too much space with his stuff in her apartment and his body in her bed. She's annoyed by his constant presence on her couch, is allegedly terrified he's going to find out she's clumsy, stubborn and can't cook, embarrassed that she dropped tomato sauce all over herself, doesn't want to give him so much as a drawer in her apartment, and yet suddenly decides to let him move completely out his hovel into her apartment anyway. I'm pretty sure I know where this is heading.

Best Quote: "I could have told you that. He took you ice-skating for god's sake." Samantha to Carrie, after Carrie tells her that her latest man is bisexual.

Questionable Plot Point: Fairly sure that smoking on an ice rink is absolutely forbidden, even in the 90s.

5 "No Ifs, Ands, or Butts"

Carrie finally decides to give up smoking, for a man. (Any reason is good enough for me). Charlotte dates a disgusting face-licker. Samantha tries to be African-American but doesn't get away with it. Steve continues to irritate Miranda by acting like a child and having no respect for her pressing career.

Carrie visits a furniture store owned by a furniture designer: Aiden, who will become the next dude in the long, long line-up that is Carrie's Relationships. Aiden is tall, handsome and charming. He's given an early warning about Carrie's ethics when she lies about being a designer just so she can get a discount on his furniture (another thing she can't afford), then later confesses that she lied, so she could con Aiden out of a few dollars. Instead of being disgusted and getting the hell away, Aiden continues to show an interest in her until she pulls out one of her filthy cancer sticks and starts puffing away. If being ripped off by a trashy column writer doesn't turn him off, that sure does. Carrie tries to tell him she's not really addicted and only smokes "a little", but fortunately he's not that stupid, telling her he has a "thing" about it and can't continue seeing her.

Carrie bitches to the SATC girls about how smoking is more important to her than some cute guy. Finally, we see some good advice given to the often clueless Carrie from the SATC girls, who are appalled that she has decided to let smoking get in the way of good things. Carrie is furious to be told that no one likes her habit and takes her bitching to Stanford, a fellow smoker, who's sure to understand. But Stanford is in the midst of his own dilemma.

Stanford has taken up company with the gayest man he has ever met, who owns an enormous…. doll collection, spread all over his bed. There's gay… and then there's *gay*. Stanford spends a bit of time considering whether the doll collection is a deal breaker (they have *names*, for goodness sakes) and decides he'll live with it. Unfortunately he's a bit too careless with one of the dollies and accidentally kicks it off the bed, smashing its porcelain face, when throwing the doll collector down in the heat of passion. So it's bye-bye, Dolly.

Meantime, Charlotte is dating a bad kisser, and by bad I mean someone who actually licks and slurps on the whole lower half of her face. Instead of telling him to stop, Charlotte sees him again, this time letting him give her face a proper washing. She decides that the subtle approach (guiding him gently and dropping hints) isn't working and flees the scene, but not before he's given her face an actual rash. #gross

Samantha starts dating a lovely African American man called Chivon with a hot bod (although the bedroom scenes are a bit blech – calling Samantha soft and sweet surely is taking it a bit far). The problem is, Chivon has a racist, interfering sister Adeena who can't stand the thought of her brother with a white woman. Instead of just shutting her mouth and waiting for it to fizzle out (and she wouldn't have had to wait long) Adeena steps in and destroys Samantha's chances with Chivon, telling Samantha that she'd better back off because Chivon ain't allowed to date no white woman. And Chivon actually lets this happen – like his sister owns him. The fact that a grown up man can let his sister sabotage his relationships based on such overt racism in the 90s is far fetched, but at least Samantha did get to experience a big African American cock. Also, Samantha picks up two new words: dis and whack, so it's not all bad.

Steve gets a chance to win a million dollars if he can make a half court shot (I think I know what that means, kinda). Miranda shows a vague interest, knowing that it's most unlikely that Steve will win the million, but Steve is convinced he's going to make the shot and tries to get Miranda excited about it. Sadly for him, she's much less interested in fairytales than in her workload, which although can be oppressive at times, does actually pay the bills. Steve becomes annoyingly petulant at her lack of interest in his half court shot and they fight about it. Message to Steve: don't dis Miranda's career. That's just whack.

6 "Are We Sluts?"

Carrie completely forgets about the last time she got snarky with a man for wanting to wait a little while before sex. Miranda is obligated to tell Steve and some of her other past 42 lovers that she's got chlamydia. Samantha's whoring about finally catches up with her and she has to move buildings to somewhere where she won't be shamed.

Charlotte has sex with a man who can't control his potty mouth when he finishes.

Carrie and Aiden go on several very enjoyable dates but after about 11 days, he still hasn't accepted her subtle invitations to come inside her apartment and have sex with her. As usual she frets about this, making it all about her, and asks the SATC girls for advice, which will prove dangerous, as it has done before and will do again. Samantha scares Carrie by telling her that if she doesn't hurry things along, she will be friendzoned.

I was hoping that someone would remind Carrie that the last time she hurried a man to make his move before he was ready, he ended up drunk in the street, stripping himself naked and waking all the neighbours. Instead the SATC girls all jump in with possible answers as to why Aiden would possibly make a girl wait more than 11 days before he bonks her. Charlotte, who always pretends that she prefers to wait 144 dates before sex, does absolutely nothing to reassure Carrie that waiting patiently and letting the man lead is the best course of action.

So Carrie takes out her confusion by getting all cranky with Aiden, who calms her down with a bubble bath and the promise of romance and sex – if she can wait for it. He's a patient man all right, as we will see.

Funnily enough it's Miranda, not Samantha, who discovers she has an STD and is advised to make a list of all her past sexual partners so she can contact them all (although presumably she could stop the calls as soon as she found the culprit). She has an hilarious conversation with the guy who actually gave it to her – the arrogant lawyer from several episodes ago, who knew he had the STD but didn't bother to inform his partners. He may be a dickhead, but at least he's honest and admits to his liability. In making her list, Miranda and Steve discover that they have slept with over 100 people between them – and that's just a lowball estimate – it does make me wonder what Samantha's list would look like. Actually…. I don't really want to know.

Speaking of Samantha, we are treated to a montage of the men she's brought home to her classy apartment in the recent past, including a scene in the lift where she openly gropes a man's crotch while standing inches from one of the other building-dwellers. Of course all this behaviour catches up with her when she buzzes in some random guy in the middle of the night, who is closely followed by a gunman – a *gunman*! Did he actually shoot anyone? But that detail is not important. What is important is that Samantha is made to feel like a slut by her prim aging neighbours who more or less evict her with their scathing opinions of her nocturnal activities. So she's off to a meat-packing district, because changing your slutty lifestyle to suit your neighbours? Ain't nobody got time for that.

Charlotte is repeatedly humiliated by her latest, who has a foul mouth of his own when he comes – calling Charlotte all manner of horrible names and then feigning complete lack of recall when she queries him about it. Liar! Another deal breaker for Charlotte. Next.

7 "Drama Queens"

Miranda gets off on domesticity and doing Steve's laundry, until she finds a skid mark. Samantha has sex with an unethical doctor. Charlotte, in the spirit of "build it and they will come" announces that this is the year she will get married. Carrie sets her neuroses on trying to ruin the perfection of her relationship with Aiden.

Carrie, who even brags that "parents love me" because she's "adorable", baulks at meeting Aiden's parents. This is after she took extreme risks to see Big's mother after he had warned her to stay away, and happily met all of Vaughn's family at once without even planning to do so.

Carrie. You're a famous writer. You network all the time, give public speeches, meet famous actors. And you're in your 30s – you're a grown up. Why so scared? And is it really necessary to bother Aiden while he's hard at work, selling his furniture to customers, to tell him that you can't meet his parents because you've got better things to do, and additionally explain that you've thought about the future of the relationship and it will just be too difficult for his parents to get over the loss of you if they break up, so it's best you and they don't meet? This is about 57 different kinds of crazy.

In the meantime, Carrie boringly agonises over the relationship with the SATC girls because it's … perfect. Just like the episode where she trashed her last "perfect" guy's apartment searching through all his private stuff, ruining any chance of seeming like a well-adjusted sort of person, she questions Aiden endlessly about his faults and hidden baggage. Aiden is terribly patient about it all, although it is relevant to note that he doesn't offer her a key to his apartment so she can get in there and sieve through it. Don't ever give her a key, Aiden.

Meanwhile, Samantha dates a guy who takes Viagra for fun, even though he doesn't need it. He's a doctor, so this seems a bit wrong. Should a qualified doctor know better than to take prescription medication unnecessarily, especially when there's a threat of unwelcome side effects? He even negligently gives one to Samantha and she becomes addicted to the thrill of it. He may as well have given her a jellybean; the effect Viagra has on women is as a placebo only, because women don't have penises. It could also be said that Samantha isn't exactly in need of a medical sexual aid. Nevertheless, the placebo effect is obviously strong, because Samantha decides she is addicted (she's not). Heaven help us all if Viagra did actually work on Samantha. There's not enough time in each episode for that.

Charlotte has been taking advice from a book for single women looking for a husband (she could do worse, I suppose) which advises her to spend more time with married couples, because they are allegedly a source of unmarried men. Who writes this guff? Charlotte immediately meets up with a married couple she knows and begs them to introduce her to a single man they know. Any one will do. And they happen to know one, by the name of Phil, so before the evening is out Charlotte has mentally inscribed his name on the wedding napkins before she's even so much as met the guy.

It all ends in tears of course, for a little while, as the married friend of Phil decides he'd rather cheat on his wife with Charlotte so refuses to set her up with Phil. But while Charlotte is running out of a bar to get away from this unfortunate turn of events, she nearly gets hit by a cab which carries none other than Trey, who meets her three criteria, especially the money one. Let the fun and hilarity start.

Carrie chews gum throughout an operatic performance and then panics when she spies Big and Natasha sitting in the same seats as them, on the other side of the theatre. What a coincidence. She runs, leaving Charlotte alone to finish being at the opera by herself. That's two bits of bad behaviour right there (gum, ditching Charlotte). She then wakes up Miranda in the middle of the night with a phone call during a freakout about seeing Big. That's strike three. And you're out, Carrie.

Miranda settles into a rut with Steve, which includes doing his disgusting laundry and clipping her toenails in bed after 6 minute sex. Are you jealous?

8 "The Big Time"

We get the first hint that Big's second marriage may be in trouble. Samantha worries about getting old. Steve, who's quite childish himself, begs Miranda to have a baby with him. (Remember this for later episodes). Charlotte is boring about Trey.

I almost feel some sympathy for Carrie here, stuck on a boring boat with boring Trey and Charlotte harping on about how they met. Trey does possess a good set of abs, but he's as interesting as a bowl of All Bran, which makes him a pretty good match for Charlotte. And then when Carrie finally manages to get away from the tedium of hearing about how they met, again, she bumps into none other than Big, her emotional black hole, who hasn't brought Natasha with him. He wants to know if they can have a conversation, but doesn't get the hint when Carrie keeps walking away from him.

Miranda and Steve, who were blissfully having sex on the washing machine during the wash cycle last episode, are suddenly in a "shitty place". Man, that went downhill fast. It all starts when Steve starts bugging Miranda about having a baby (I too would find that inappropriate and annoying), continues when Steve watches cartoons made for 6 year olds on high volume (irritating and juvenile) and ends with Steve persuading Miranda to get a puppy of all things (does Miranda not remember Charlotte trying this one, albeit for different reasons? It was only last season). The cute puppy is the final straw, and instead of bringing them together and practising for a real baby, it tips Miranda over the edge and she basically tells Steve it's over. I feel sorry for the puppy, mostly.

The only thing worth mentioning further about Trey is that Charlotte makes him wait for any kind of sexual contact until he professes to love her, after which she relents with a hand job. At least she's sticking to the Rule of 144 with this one.

Big makes contact with Carrie by phone and then with a random drop-in to tell her that he's missing her and can't stop thinking about her. (Thank goodness we have messaging for this sort of stuff now). You can tell it's going to get messy, can't you? Speaking of messy, Samantha has sex with a slimy neighbour, believing him to be her last chance at sex now that she's five days late with her period and is premenopausal, meaning that no hot guy will ever want to fuck her again. I don't understand where the SATC girls get their irrational ideas from, but at times like this they really do give women a bad name generally. Thankfully, her period arrives mid-sex on some very expensive sheets and while the sleazy man is disgusted, Samantha is thrilled. I really think she could have offered to get those sheets dry-cleaned, though. It would have been a nice gesture.

Best Quote: Samantha, telling the girls "I'm a little…older… than you".

9 "Easy Come, Easy Go"

Big keeps popping into Carrie's life to tease her with the notion that he might be leaving his wife. Samantha conducts a scientific experiment with her man's sperm. Charlotte is intrigued, not concerned, at how Trey seems to let his mother make his decisions for him. Miranda breaks up with Steve but is immediately jealous when he meets another woman within minutes.

Charlotte finally gets herself engaged, but does it all wrong of course. (Spoiler alert: she does almost the same thing when it comes to her second engagement with Harry. Do these girls never learn?) Bunny, Trey's prissy and controlling mother, seems to have Trey wrapped around her little finger, making suggestions to Trey about all manner of things while he amiably agrees with his catchphrase "Alrighty". Charlotte should have received huge warning bells here. Bunny is clearly going to make some very difficult mother-in-law material with her snobby, bossy character. But Charlotte has too many stars in her eyes to make an informed decision about whether marrying Trey is a good idea, and suggests to him that they get hitched. He's so weak that he mildly agrees to it and boom! that's the engagement story Charlotte will have to tell her grandchildren, which although could be over 40 years away if ever, is a story Charlotte can't possibly accept.

Thank goodness Charlotte is able to overwrite history when Trey later does the right thing by offering to buy her the most beautiful ring at Tiffany's. I'm a bit jealous, but only about the ring.

Steve is in the process of moving out of Miranda's apartment and at least she has the grace to feel a bit guilty about it, offering to help him find a new one. After all, they've only lived together about 2 weeks (seems like) and he now has a puppy to take with, which will rule him out for quite a few rentals I would assume. Steve continues to be annoying though, by staying out all night without even telling Miranda so she's left in charge of the puppy, and giving random females Miranda's home number so they can call Steve and leave messages on her voicemail. So, so tacky! Couldn't he have waited a little while? It's a credit to Miranda that she handles this so well. I would have expected her to be furious but for some reason she is only resigned, and a little bit jealous. (She does have this strange habit of getting rid of men and then being all uncomfortable when they meet other women.)

In another classic case of wanting what he can't have, Big gets drunk (at a furniture designer showcase? Really?) and decides to pursue Carrie and let her in on a secret: his marriage is not working out. The only reason he can give is that it's all a bit beige, and Carrie tries her best to appear uncaring and uninterested but after a few false starts they find themselves in bed together by the end of the episode. My question is this: Carrie was finding it very hard to concentrate while Aiden renovates her apartment, so she books a hotel room at the Stanhope so she can type out her trashy column. Hasn't she ever heard of a library? Or a park? Those would have been free, which for a person on a budget would have been ideal. She's not writing a symphony here.

Ironically, it is Aiden who innocently directs Big to find Carrie in her hotel lobby, chase her into the lift and then to her room, where they begin their affair. See what I mean? She would have been able to finish her column in a library.

In perhaps what is the biggest overshare ever to appear on SATC – and I think this trumps Charlotte's cunt painting – Samantha informs the girls that her current man has the "funkiest tasting spunk". Carrie is quite right when she suggests Samantha discusses this problem with "no-one". After all Samantha, no one asked. You had other options: don't give blow jobs. Don't swallow. Dump him. But for some reason Samantha decides to tinker with nature and get her man to try some vegan potion which she hopes will reduce the PH of his jizz… and thanks for the research Sam, because we all now know not to bother.

10 "All or Nothing"

Carrie and Big continue to have sex on the sly, with Carrie confessing to both Samantha and Miranda (but sensibly, not to Charlotte). Samantha moves house but then gets the flu. Miranda has phone sex but it becomes problematic. Charlotte decides that the McDougall pre-nup puts her value way too low.

During a celebration of Samantha's new ubercool apartment in the meatpacking district where you can swear at the neighbours and they'll swear back at you, Charlotte bores everyone about Trey again and how life isn't worth living until you have a good man, and raves about how awesome her mother-in-law to be is. She's about to get a few rude shocks, the first later in the episode and then plenty more later on. After the party, Carrie hangs about to confess her Big affair to Samantha, who is more or less fine with it, as she's been having sex with married men for decades so she's completely normalised. Carrie begs Samantha to slap some sense into her, but Samantha refuses to pass judgement. Wrong audience, Carrie.

Carrie realises that the only way to avoid continuation of the affair is just to stay near Aiden, but he's off out of town for a while, so she invites Big into her bed. He doesn't like it though, because it smells of another man, so he'll only be doing her in hotels from now on. Well - as long as he pays. Carrie waits until the last possible second before Aiden gets back to replace the sheets, so she's in the middle of stripping them as he walks in the door. She really leaves things to the last minute, doesn't she? Aiden chooses this moment to tell her he loves her – which is ironic because Samantha said that until he said that to her, Carrie belongs to no one. This is some twisted logic from Samantha.

Charlotte is delivered a prenup by Trey in a casual offhand way, mixed in with the engagement party guest list. Naturally she is stunned but in Trey's part of the world, that's all very routine. Welcome to the world of the uber-rich, Charlotte, it's what you wanted, right? The prenup doesn't meet with her expectations though – it only values her at half a million and that's after 30 years of wedded bliss. Clearly even Charlotte doesn't think this marriage will last, because on Miranda's advice she decides to challenge her future mother in law about it and demand a million in the event of divorce after any length of time. And for some reason Bunny actually gives in, and Charlotte signs it and the wedding's back on. Charlotte even manages to get the $1,300 china pattern she wants. It seems she was a born gold digger.

The girls walk home from the posh engagement party, minus Charlotte because she now belongs to Trey. They muse about how unbelievable it is that she's actually going to marry this boring prat, and Miranda comments that Charlotte's only getting a tenth of what she's worth in the prenup. There are so many things wrong with this statement it's hard to know where to start. Why is Charlotte valued at $10 million just because she marries someone? Why should the value mean anything at all if marriage is forever? Unless there are children produced in the marriage, why should Charlotte stand to profit from it if it ends, given that she is able to support herself?

In other fairly uninteresting plotlines, Miranda has phone sex but the guy is holding two dirty conversations at once and she catches him out. Samantha gets the flu.

Carrie suddenly and irrationally takes Aiden's dog for a walk, in stilettos, so she can meet Big, who's dropped over at her apartment unannounced – again – and after a fight with Big on the street, the dog runs off. Hours later, Carrie still hasn't been able to find him. Amazingly, the dog beats her home, managing to find her apartment building, ascend the stairs and get through the front door, trot up the stairs/catch the lift, find the correct door and knock on it so that Aiden can let him in. Also, Aiden doesn't even wonder how his dog did this. Carrie is on the verge of confessing her Big affair when Aiden accuses her of cheating – but she is visibly relieved when she discovers it's her smoking he's accusing her of. I'm not sure where she got the cigarette from, given she flew out of her apartment without money nor fags, nor how she kept the cigarette alight in the pouring rain ... but these are things we will never ever know.

11 "Running With Scissors"

Carrie and Big decide to continue their affair at his place instead of a hotel, to avoid getting caught by people they know. So instead they get caught by Big's wife. Samantha has an HIV test and then has sex in a swing. Miranda is offended by a man-sandwich. Charlotte is boring about her upcoming wedding.

Who knew you could hire someone to find a wedding dress for you? Who knew Charlotte didn't have the time to do that herself? At least it saves the SATC girls the grim task of having to wade through Charlotte's colour coded tags on her bridal magazine collection; there's a few hours you'd never get back.

In the ultimate way to waste her husband's money, Charlotte hires bitchy gay Anthony to sit with her in a high-class wedding dress shop so he can be thoroughly nasty to the poor sales girl, who couldn't possibly be getting paid enough for this. Even her advice to Charlotte about whether white would suit her skin tone is rudely interrupted by Anthony, and Charlotte, who considers herself a princess of impeccable breeding, does zero to stop him nor does she even show embarrassment. I would have fired him on the spot. What's wrong with getting one or two of your bridesmaids to come to a couple of shops with you so they can sip champagne while you try on a few frocks? Oh, that's right – they're sick of hearing about it already.

Fortunately, Charlotte finds the perfect dress in under four minutes after being shown a mere rack and half of them, and selects it before trying it or any other dress on. I thought Charlotte would be a little fussier about all this but I'm glad she's not because the less of Anthony the better. I wonder how much he earned for his four minutes?

In a woeful plotline for Miranda, she is asked by a man in a sandwich suit on the street to "eat me". It's funny. He's a sandwich, and he's advertising a sandwich shop. But instead of drawing upon her limited sense of humour, Miranda goes all snowflake and accuses the shop owner of sexual harassment. Doesn't she know what sexual harassment is? It isn't that.

Samantha is momentarily distracted from her ... rich ... sex life, when Tom, a man who is announced as the male version of her, asks her for a fuck, takes her to his apartment, dry humps her and *then* asks her if she's had an HIV test. It may have been a better idea to ask her this before taking her to his apartment – less time wasted that way, perhaps. Tom shows Samantha an actual swing he has set up in his bedroom and taunts her with how fantastic it's going to be, after her HIV test.

We are then treated to Samantha's angst over the test: discussing it with the girls, counting up her conquests in front of the nurse, fainting in the clinic when it comes time for results. But my question is this. Is sex on a swing really that great? How do you manage the actual ... how to put this .. thrusting? I would imagine it's impossible and a little frustrating. It's a crappy swing anyway; it doesn't even hold the two of them, crashing to the floor with them both in it. You can't tell me that wouldn't hurt. A lot.

The Big affair comes to an abrupt and tragic end, especially the bit where Natasha loses a tooth. But let's go back a bit.

The cat is firmly out of the bag when Charlotte catches Carrie and Big exiting a hotel together. Seems the hotel was coincidentally eerily close to the tailor where Charlotte is having her wedding dress fittings. Charlotte is onto the pair right away, even though Big does his best to rescue the situation. He might have got away with it too, had Carrie not given the jig up completely with a face exactly like the cat caught with its paw in the cream.

Carrie promises Charlotte that she's ending the affair. This is the third time Carrie has said this and not meant it; what she means is she'll try to hide it better next time. And by this she means visiting Big's apartment next time (because that somehow lowers the risk) where they argue about telling their respective partners about the whole mess (Natasha will save Big the trouble in mere moments). Imagine leaving Carrie in your bed while you go back to work, where she is free to wander about assessing your furniture and décor, then letting your wife discover her with wet hair racing out the back door. It all ends in tears of course, most of them probably Natasha's as her modelling career is ruined for a while after she smashes a tooth in a fall while racing after Carrie. As usual, Carrie makes it all about her by musing "I had found a way to let myself out of the mess". It's a really odd way to describe being caught red-handed, blowing your lover's marriage to bits and putting his wife in hospital. I would have said something like "what a day. Thank goodness that's over".

12 "Don't Ask, Don't Tell"

Miranda tries speed dating so she won't have to be alone at Charlotte's wedding. Samantha has sex with the groomsmen, who speaks with such a strong Scottish accent she can't tell what he he's saying (another of Samantha's non-requirements in a man: being able to understand him). Carrie waits until precisely the worst moment to confess her Big affair to Aiden. Charlotte is horrified to discover she's about to marry a man who's boring AND impotent.

Carrie agonises over whether to tell Aiden about Big, because the damage that's already been done isn't quite sufficient. Miranda says yes, Samantha says no. Charlotte blocks all this talk of infidelity during her wedding "week": she really cements her position as Bridezilla Extraordinaire this episode. Samantha has a fight with Charlotte during the bridesmaidal dress fitting because the dress isn't short enough. Charlotte tells her she can't possibly wear her dress up around her see-you-next-Tuesday and then explains in sign language exactly what that means (c-u-n-t). It's so cute that *Charlotte* needs to explain this wonderful little acronym to *Samantha*.

Anyway. Miranda is successful at attracting a man to her honeypot at speed dating, but she does it by pretending she's an air hostess, because all the guys are completely turned off by her being a lawyer. I will never get this: why would a man turn down meeting a smart, high earning woman who he can potentially have a smart, high earning marriage with? Regardless, Miranda keeps up the pretence of her fake career by wearing an actual necktie to their date (because air hostesses like to wear their uniforms outside of work) and also by adopting what I assume is an "air hostess accent" – a sort of breathy, high pitched, flirty tone. Before the week is out she's already having sex with this ER doctor called Harris. Aiden is very unimpressed at Miranda's deception and tells her in no uncertain terms that it will cause issues in a future relationship, which worries Carrie enormously because she's about to fuck up everything by confessing about the Big affair.

Aiden doesn't need to worry about Miranda though. Her date was a liar too, and a bigger one than she - he works at a sports store – so Miranda ditches him right there. Wouldn't it have been great if Miranda had confessed too, making them even? She may have had a date to the wedding after all.

Samantha targets the Scottish groomsman, deciding he will be her next conquest. He doesn't speak American so she's a bit bamboozled by him, but of course that's no impediment for Samantha and she's onto him like butter on bread.

Charlotte drunkenly admits to the girls that she can't wait to fuck Trey, meaning she hasn't yet, and they are horrified to receive this piece of information that hasn't yet come up in dozens of tedious conversations about Trey before now. What a thing to keep secret, given that sex is the first, second, third and last topic on the SATC girls' plates at every lunch meeting! I'm as stunned as they are. Samantha warns Charlotte that this could be a huge mistake, which turns out to be quite prophetic as Trey admits to impotence the night before the wedding to a drunken but much crestfallen Charlotte.

It's the wedding! Carrie confesses her Big affair to Aiden right before she's due at the church, so Aiden more or less dumps her on the spot, leaving her alone to counsel Charlotte in her $14,000 dress about whether Trey jerked off last night before she turned up unannounced, or whether he really is properly impotent. Charlotte has already told Carrie that she doesn't want her fighting with Aiden at her wedding, so I wonder what sort of trouble Carrie was in later for not bringing him at all? That was a $250 dinner that went to waste.

Charlotte decides to put thoughts of flaccid penises aside for now, and go through with the wedding seeing as it's been quite a bit of work to prepare and she is 34 after all. Carrie tries to talk Aiden back into a relationship after he turns up to tell her it's over. Through her tears, the SATC girls have the photoshoot with the bride on the steps of the church, Charlotte oblivious to the angst of the previous couple of hours. I hope Carrie's red eyes didn't ruin her photo album.

Best quote: The perfect wedding: "Charlotte had something old, something new, something borrowed, and someone Samantha blew."

13 "Escape from New York"

Matthew McConaughey wants to make a film of Carrie's columns. The SATC girls minus barely married Charlotte go to LA so Carrie can meet him. Trey is uninterested in sex (which is quite different to being impotent and represents a whole new problem for the marriage). Miranda feels the need to mount a mechanical bull. Charlotte is boring about golf.

Charlotte arrives back from her honeymoon and saps everyone's patience with golfing pictures, because that's all they did on their honeymoon. Trey won't touch her, and she and Carrie compare their respective miseries over coffee. Carrie is preparing to go to LA with Samantha and Miranda, and Charlotte is a bit miffed at not being able to go (I wasn't aware being married meant no more girly weekends).

In LA, Carrie has a meeting with Matthew McConaughey, whom I've always rated. But in this episode, it's hard to figure out whether he is playing himself as he really is, or if he's deliberately adding a nutjob element to his character to make himself seem more intense and dimensional. Either way, it is absolutely frightening. It's like he's taken some kind of substance; leaping about yelling rhetorical questions, insulting Carrie and swearing, dropping into his interpretation of the character of Big, whom he seems intent on recreating in a kind of aggressive, creepy way. It's all very unnerving and I'm not sure what the point was of making McConaughey look like a loon. Maybe the reason was to put Carrie off ever meeting him again, blowing a chance at having a movie made about her life (but at least there's SATC the movies 1 and 2 coming up, so all is not lost).

Meanwhile, Samantha meets an LA porn industry star with a huge penis who works as a dildo model (and I've learned something here because I had no idea they used actual penises to make these things). Unfortunately he's also a poet and general thoughtful sort of guy who shows an interest in Samantha that goes beyond merely having sex with her. This is another thing on Samantha's list of things not required in a man: treating her as if she was a whole person and not just a one-nighter; so he's quickly set free.

Miranda meets a guy too, but he loses interest in her suddenly while they are in the middle of a conversation. Miranda suffers a crisis of confidence, feeling invisible and in need of validation. She achieves this validation by leaping on a mechanical bull in a bar, but sadly her act follows a sexy young woman who looks right at home on a bull, whereas Miranda looks like a lawyer temporarily set free from a pile of affidavits, even after she rips her shirt open to show everyone her bra.

Back in NY, Charlotte continues to try to consummate her marriage, but in addition to being impotent Trey just has no desire either. It's a double whammy. I don't know how Charlotte gets away with attaching a ring of stamps around his penis while he's asleep and then removing it before he wakes up in an attempt to see whether he gets night stiffies. He must have no feeling there at all.

14 "Sex and Another City"

Still in LA, Carrie is deceived and thoroughly embarrassed by a guy who lies about his job, residence and celebrity connections. Charlotte joins the girls in LA after deciding that she'd rather ogle real men than spend another minute trying to get Trey interested. Miranda meets an old ex-NY friend who has gone to extreme lengths to lose weight and embrace the LA lifestyle. The girls go to a party at the Playboy Mansion, which is for some reason a bucket list item for Samantha. Charlotte and Carrie experience the Full Brazilian for the first time. The less said about that the better.

Samantha gets stars in her eyes and drool on her lips when she sees Hugh Hefner across the room at a movie premiere after party that she's somehow got into with Carrie, despite the female bouncer's best efforts to keep them out. I don't understand why Samantha would select Hugh Hefner, a crusty old pervert surrounded by plastic women half Samantha's age, to be someone she would aspire to spend time with. For one thing, who wants to spend their evening with his ever-present hangers-on; a bunch of 20-year-old girls who all look exactly the same, fawning over their sugar daddy and vying for his attention? Is this anyone's idea of a good night out? Or does Samantha just want to have sex with Hefner, and in which case why? Is he particularly attractive to Samantha? Does she just want to be able to brag about it afterwards? I also find it hard to believe that she just wants to get to know him as a person, because that's not ever on Samantha's agenda.

Without a solution to that mystery, the girls carry on their little LA mini break with Charlotte, who arrives sexually frustrated and ready to be picked up by anybody with a decent body and a bit of charm. One such contender chats her up at the Playboy Mansion party, thanks to Samantha who gets them all an invite. Even though Charlotte is scathing of Carrie's fling with Big, she is more than comfortable getting cosy and not just a little bit drunk and flirtatious with a random by the poolside.

Luckily he insults her by offering to increase her breast size (I wonder what he wanted in terms of compensation for that?) and she storms off. We can but guess where that might have ended if Charlotte had been OK with a complete stranger paying for her boob job.

Miranda meets up with an old NY friend who has been thoroughly LA-fied to the point where he chews but does not swallow his steak. Apparently that's the LA method for losing weight. Miranda is appalled and runs away as fast as she can, back to NY where good steak is enjoyed and no one speaks of taking hikes in the wilderness.

Carrie meets Keith at the movie launch party who flatters her by telling her she's too pretty to be a writer and compliments her brand of cigarettes. He then goes to great lengths to impress her further by telling her he's Matt Damon's agent, and the next day taking her to a viewing of a multi-million dollar apartment for sale that he's thinking of buying; but he really didn't need to go that far to get Carrie to have sex with him. She was a goner the moment he took her into the VIP club at the party to meet celebrities.

Keith walks her back to "his" house, they have a sleepover, then Carrie Fisher walks in on them the next morning and it blows up most spectacularly in their faces: he's a big fat liar, using his employer's place and passing it off as his own in addition to all his other bull. You can't trust anyone, can you, especially in LA. Setting up a fake viewing at a multi-million dollar property just to impress a girl is certainly taking things a little bit far. What a phony! The whole episode seems to be having a dig at LA in its entirety: food, parties, shopping and especially its citizens. It's a good thing they aren't different countries or there probably would have been a war kicked off by these plotlines.

15 "Hot Child in the City"

Miranda gets braces, an odd solution to the tongue-thrusting problem she's been diagnosed with. Charlotte catches Trey pleasuring himself and is not pleased. We discover that Batmitzvahs can cost a million dollars. Carrie meets another man who lies to her about real estate.

The oddest thing about Charlotte catching Trey masturbating is not that he's doing it – and as a sexually educated woman in the 90s she should have realised that masturbation is not sex, therefore there was no need to be so shocked – it's the *way* he was doing it. Watch carefully and you will note that he is thrusting against the bathroom cabinet like it has a vagina in it. Really, male masturbation is more of a "hand" action than a "pelvis" action: he's doing it wrong. Just saying.

Also, it's weird that Trey allowed Charlotte to catch him not just once but twice, the second time doing it noisily in their ensuite while she's *awake in the bedroom*, browsing through a mag/book/whatever and smirking with glee, because she's replaced all the model's heads in the *Juggs* magazine Trey is "using" with her own head. She's complete with a virginal veil because they're unused proofs from their wedding album. Doesn't she know that Trey's not looking at the faces in those pages?

Back to Miranda and her braces. Aside from the fact that braces are a solution for crooked or buck teeth, not tongue thrusting, I've never seen someone get quite so much food stuck in the front top wires during a meal. I personally had braces for five years and the worst thing that happened to me was a bit of apple skin perched in there now and then. It looks like Miranda practically rubbed a piece of chocolate mud cake into the front of her teeth. Coupled with this and the humiliation she experiences when told by a 13 year old that her braces are the "old" kind because they aren't sapphire, it's all the incentive Miranda needs to have those braces ripped off again after she's barely worn them a week. Thousands of dollars down the drain, not to mention the fact that the tongue thrusting is never heard of again. Another plotline raised, then put to death in under 25 minutes, leaving a multitude of unanswered questions.

Samantha somehow picks up a new client who is a precocious, spoiled and horrendously outspoken 13 year old Jewish girl. I was wondering how Samantha got this client, as she seems so different from her usual clientele. But then I realised I don't really know who Samantha's clientele usually are, apart from Smarmy Richard (who'll turn up later). So maybe Samantha normally does PR for spoiled rich teenagers. Anyway. Samantha comes face to face with the demanding brat and learns a valuable life lesson: it's stupid to be threatened by 13 year old girls who have it all, because what they are really missing out on is a childhood. Or maybe they are just having a different childhood to the one you got, Samantha. Regardless, it's not worth losing any sleep over.

Carrie tries to get her shoes fixed at her favourite shoe repair shop (ie. the shoes she's wearing. If they need fixing, why is she wearing them? Does this remind you of *Seinfeld*; the time Kramer went to return some pants – the very pants he was wearing? And Elaine asks him to consider what he was planning on wearing home and he says it hardly matters because he never got to the shop to return them? Tee hee). Same thing happens here, in that Carrie can't get her shoes fixed because there's a comic book shop where her shoe guy used to be. So instead she manages to hook up with the comic bookstore owner: a cute longhaired guy called Wade, who lives with his parents in an expensive apartment that he tries to pass off as his own. What is it with these guys who lie about where they are living? This is the second one in a row now. Even though Samantha is appalled that Carrie is seeing a guy who lives with mummy and daddy and tells Carrie to dump him immediately "Here. Use my cell phone", Carrie decides she quite likes having parents run about after her, serving her cookies and dinner. As she doesn't appear to have parents of her own, I do get this. However, Wade's lies cross the line when he drops Carrie in the poo by pinning his big bag of dope on her so he won't get into trouble with Mummy. And Carrie seizes the opportunity, taking the dope and never seeing the freeloader again. You go, girl.

We attend another couple of sessions of therapy: this time it's Charlotte's turn, as she attempts to crack Trey's ongoing resistance to making love to her. This therapist is not much better than any other therapist we've seen on SATC: this one suggests the couple name their private parts in a non-threatening manner so they can talk about them without embarrassment while sharing sexual fantasies. Are any of these therapists actually qualified?

Questionable Plot Point: Why, when Carrie gives Miranda's number to a cute guy who's been checking Miranda out, does he respond by giving Carrie his card and telling her to tell Miranda to call him? That's not how it works, dude.

Another Questionable Plot Point: Where on earth does Wade manage to get a scooter from at the end of his first date with Carrie? It literally just appears out of nowhere.

16 "Frenemies"

For some unknown reason, Carrie is given a public speaking gig as an expert on "How to Find Love". Trey continues to resist all of Charlotte's efforts to consummate their marriage. Charlotte and Samantha clash over their respective attitudes towards sex. The girls seem to run out of men to date in NY, as Miranda considers one of Carrie's exes despite being given a stern warning to steer clear.

Is Carrie's presentation to a room full of single women the worst presentation you've ever seen? No wonder they wanted their money back. It seems that Carrie didn't prepare even a single sentence of what she was going to say. She rabbits on for a couple of minutes about men being available all over the city, and then grins like "that's it. That's all I got".

As an educated writer, surely she could have prepared a proper, meaningful presentation including some helpful tips such as how to approach a man you don't know, some ideas on what to wear, the topics men are interested in, how to achieve confidence around men, how not to appear too desperate, and how to steer clear of unsuitable men. It's unbelievable that after this first appalling seminar, Carrie then has to present a *second* one – to the same bunch of women who bothered to come back, and not learning from her mistake the first time around, has absolutely no idea what to say to them this time either. Dearie me.

Miranda is stood up by her date, and instead of calling him when he's oh; I don't know, 30 minutes late, she waits *three hours* to call him, making sure she is well and truly fuming and in no mood for a reasonable explanation (such as that he died. Which as it turns out, he actually did). I can only be thankful that we now live in an era where Miranda would never have had to yell at a dead man's mother, because she'd just message the guy asking what's up, and see that he hadn't received the message so know that she probably wasn't being ghosted. Also, if a guy does stand you up without a reasonable explanation, we now know it's much cooler to shrug it off instead of yelling at the guy's mother about it. At least, I hope most women appreciate this.

As a result of Miranda's date dying and her subsequent over-reaction, she is weak enough to fall for the next guy she meets, who happens to be a fairly arrogant arsehole named Jim, who dated Carrie eight years ago. Carrie is quick to issue a strong steer-clear-of-the-arsehole warning, which Miranda blindly ignores and accepts an offer to go on a date with him. Carrie is appalled, but not appalled enough to resist the chance to go out on their second date as a third wheel because Miranda can't deal with the fact that Carrie doesn't like her new man, and wants to "re-acquaint" her with arsehole Jim and see if she can't make them like each other.

I must question when this has ever been an issue with the SATC girls; especially Miranda who I generally see as the one who is most together and sane, albeit by a slim margin. When have any of them cared two bits about whether their girlfriends liked their latest shag? As the shags tend to mostly stick around for one or two episodes, it barely matters, but for the long-term ones such as Trey, Berger, smarmy Richard, Steve and of course Big, did you ever hear any SATC girl saying something like

"Can I ask you a question? As my dear friend, do you approve or disapprove of my latest chap?"

You didn't, because no one ever asked that. Plenty of times, people passed their opinions of Big, but they were unsolicited, unwelcome and can I also say largely ignored.

Regardless, Miranda gets to see the true arsehole that is Jim when he does exactly what Carrie predicted and acts like an arsehole. Touché.

The girls rarely fight, but Samantha talks up her active sex life a little too much in front of Charlotte who still isn't getting any, and Charlotte can't stand hearing about it anymore. Charlotte basically calls Samantha a slut and suggests that sex should be between two people who love each other; a concept alien to Samantha. I'm on the fence about this, and Carrie and Miranda refuse to mediate so the whole thing blows up and we have our first real SATC catfight. But it's OK because they make up and Samantha is the first person Charlotte calls when Trey manages to fuck her for 90 seconds. Because no one else cares, really.

17 "What Goes Around Comes Around"

Carrie is mugged, and makes it all about her by deciding that instead of random bad luck it's all about personal karma. Charlotte becomes deeply attracted to a gardener at Trey's family mansion and loses control of herself, which gloomily begins her separation from Trey. Miranda suffers a crisis of confidence (once more). Samantha fucks her namesake even though he's about less than half her age.

Carrie bursts into a hair salon yelling that she's been robbed, managing to swivel heads for precisely two seconds before everyone goes on with what they were doing. New York, what a great place to live. A police officer bothers to show up at the salon to take down the details of the mugging (really? I thought the police would hang up on you if you reported a mugging in NY). Miranda has also turned up with the ugliest pair of shoes she owns for Carrie to wear home, seeing as Carrie lost her Manolos as part of the theft process. It was good of Miranda to go home, select some shoes and head to the salon. But those shoes really were heinous; no wonder Carrie was nonplussed. She could have just worn the salon slippers home in the cab – she never walks or gets the bus so why bother Miranda?

But it turns out to be worth Miranda's while, sort of. She flirts blatantly with the detective who shows up to feign interest in the mugging. He gets a date with her, but he didn't bargain for SATC-girl angst. Imagining that the police officer is way out of her league (because he's so good looking), she decides to get white-girl wasted on vodka martinis during their second date. He's horrified by her drunkenness (although I note it didn't stop him from having sex with her). Miranda has yet to learn that her own sharp wit and intelligence might have been enough to keep him interested, even if she doesn't rate her own physical attractiveness highly enough.

Somehow, a whole bunch of men start calling Samantha's phone number asking for Sam Jones and gabbing on about some party he's having. Instead of having better things to do, Samantha decides to crash this party because it sounds like it might be excellent. At the very least she'll be able to meet the other Sam Jones and tell him she has the same name as him. Sounds like a really good reason to go to a party. She drags Carrie along and they are dissatisfied when they discover that it's just a nasty college gathering with a room full of boys half their age. Thankfully they have the good sense to leave it, but not before Carrie experiences her second bit of bad luck when she is pushed down some stairs resulting in a fall much like the one Natasha experienced a couple of episodes ago, but minus the broken tooth. Carrie decides this is definitely bad karma, and a strong signal that she must immediately track down Natasha and apologise in person now that Natasha's marriage is over and she was the cause.

Samantha decides to take the other Sam Jones' cherry when he turns up on her doorstep with a rose, smitten with her overt sexuality. They have a sex montage, and Sam falls in love with Samantha right there and then, even though she tells him to get out of her house now. He leaves desperate messages on her phone. Ah, love. The end.

Charlotte is so attracted to a sexy, sweaty gardener at a swanky MacDougal family get-together that she brazenly tongue kisses him right there in the yard, to be seen by her sister-in-law who obviously doesn't like Charlotte one bit as she announces the indiscretion to the whole family at happy hour. Who would have thought Bunny MacDougal, Charlotte's arch-nemesis, would have saved the day by turning the whole thing into a joke and enabling a change of subject? It's the second nicest thing Bunny ever did for Charlotte, after grudgingly valuing Charlotte at a cool million on the pre-nup. Regardless, Charlotte is in big trouble with Trey, who offers Charlotte the opportunity to continue in their sham marriage by looking the other way when she indulges herself elsewhere. Bargain! Charlotte should have agreed – let's face it, she has everything else she could ever want, and lots of marriages end up this way anyway. But Charlotte can't let go of her fairytale dream and tells Trey it's over. He answers with his customary "alrighty". Does the man possess a single emotion?

Carrie decides to pursue Natasha so she can give her lame apology and end her run of bad karma, but won't take the hint when Natasha makes it very clear she's not interested in any contact with Carrie at all. So Carrie gets what she deserves when she interrupts Natasha's lunch to cleanse her guilt. Natasha gives her a right serve, making Carrie feel about two feet tall. And for all her fussiness about finding the perfect dress to wear for the Women in the Arts thingy, Carrie wears her very skankiest backless lycra bodycon outfit. She should have worn "Women in the Arts", instead of "I'm Here to be Stepped Upon".

SMH Plot Point: Carrie actually takes a swig from the wine glass in front of her at Natasha's lunch table. Natasha was already appalled by you, Carrie.

18 "Cock a Doodle Do!"

Carrie and Miranda are unsettled to find that their exes have new girlfriends. Miranda is furious with Carrie after Carrie organises a post-marriage-breakup lunch with Big, sparking the next huge SATC spat. Trey finally manages to fuck Charlotte, now that they are living apart and about to get divorced (as usual, his timing is all wrong). Samantha is woken by some noisy transsexuals on the beat in the early hours of each morning.

The episode starts off with a strange sub-plot about roosters keeping Carrie awake in the night as they crow loudly in the early mornings in the animal hospital next to her building. Carrie requests that they be moved somewhere out of her line of hearing. The vet complies. Ok.

Another sub-plot deals with Miranda's annoyance at what she perceives is a girl at the Chinese delivery service she frequents, laughing at her for ordering the same thing all the time. As usual it's Miranda's own paranoia about what complete strangers think of her menu choices (I mean, why does she care) that causes her to overreact, storming down to the restaurant in a funk, primed to yell at the poor girl at the other end of the phone. But it turns out that the girl taking orders is a sweet, giggling young thing who seems to just really enjoy laughing a lot. Perhaps Miranda would rather a surly, sarcastic person on the other end of the phone.

The main point of this episode was to make sure that Carrie and Big are back in each other's lives, beginning with a phone call made by Big to Carrie to inform her that he has painted his bedroom wall a ghastly shade of red, Natasha has left, and does Carrie want to meet up for lunch? You bet she would. We've still got another three seasons to go, plus a couple of movies. But Miranda is most unimpressed, giving Carrie a few choice words during a shopping session and storming away after proclaiming that she's had it with Big drama. They make up with only minutes to go before Carrie's lunch date with Big, where she hopes to achieve "closure" in some form. Instead they end up falling in the nearby river together, after Carrie dodges a kiss hello and yanks Big over the edge of the path with her. This is a result of Miranda advising her to avoid kissing him, but I can't help but wonder if a public kiss on the cheek might have been all right by Miranda. It was more likely tongue kissing back at his apartment that Miranda was warning against. In any case they do end up back at his apartment for separate showers, and Carrie wears his shirt home (and little else), thus ensuring her a future meeting with Big in season 4.

There's not a lot more to say about this episode other than Samantha has a few skirmishes with some local noisy trannies outside her window in the early hours of the morning, who prove a lot more difficult to be rid of than Carrie's roosters. Samantha throws a bucket of water over them, which works initially, but they return with eggs and manage to pelt Samantha in the head with one. They also disappear after this episode, much like the roosters.

Also, Trey arrives at Charlotte's place with a sudden renewed interest in her, and actually seems to be able to get it up long enough to give it to her properly, for the first time ever. Yay! But then they have a conversation about how they got married for all the wrong reasons, and rushed into it. Which is confusing because (spoiler alert) they both completely forget about this conversation and get back together next season.

10 Times Samantha was Horrible to Smith Jarrod (which make you wonder why he stuck around)

1. When she changes his name because she thinks his birth name is stupid
2. When she refuses to hold his hand while walking along the street, preferring instead to fall and twist her ankle
3. Abandoning him at a party to go upstairs to have sex with Smarmy Richard, and allowing Smith to catch her immediately afterwards
4. Tell him he may know AA, but she knows PR (and it turns out, he was better at PR than she was)
5. Making him produce a sex tape with her to prove to the world that Samantha is the one he's banging
6. Telling him to sleep with other women while he's away, because she's not his girlfriend, and then changing her mind and telling him not to after all
7. Not telling Smith about her cancer diagnosis until after she's had the surgery, and then blurting it out to him at a movie premiere in front of paparazzi
8. Allowing him to shave his hair when hers starts to fall out, in a gesture of sympathy for her, even though she could and does wear a wig. Luckily he looks completely hot even with a number two
9. Covering herself with sushi and lying to wait for him for hours, then getting really annoyed with him because work made him late and she stupidly lay there for hours (SATC The Movie, (1))
10. Breaking up with him for no reason (also SATC The Movie, (1))

Season 4

1 "The Agony and the 'Ex'-tacy"

Charlotte is boring about Trey to a complete stranger at a party. Carrie is stood up by the whole entire guest list on her 35th birthday dinner. Samantha tries to seduce a celibate monk with three cans of peas. Miranda makes a lot of sarcastic self-deprecating jokes about her singleness. Charlotte is boring about soulmates.

Carrie's turning 35, so Samantha organises a party for her at a restaurant. Carrie turns up, a little late, wearing her strange headband, and no-one is there. About half an hour later, still no one has arrived. There are about 9 vacant seats around the table. A cake turns up. It hasn't been paid for, so Carrie gets stuck with that bill as well as the solo drinks she's had. It's not revealed who would order a cake for their close friend without paying for it, then not show at the event, but there's a friend who'd be off my Christmas card list forever. When Carrie gets home there are a few weak apologies on the machine - Miranda, Charlotte, Stanford; traffic, wrong restaurant - but no explanation from the other 6. How can nine out of nine people all have compelling and unavoidable excuses to not show up to the same party?

The girls attend an engagement party for a man they've all had various intimate moments with according to the SATC girls' personal standards: Charlotte kissed him, Miranda showed him one boob, Carrie and Samantha had sex with him. Obviously anything less than sex is not enough for the groom-to-be to remember you by, because he mixes up Miranda and Charlotte. It's weird that a guy would invite people to his engagement party when they're so distant to him that he can't remember their names.

While wandering the streets with Carrie, Samantha spies a priest outside a church and instantly (and rather immaturely) brands him "Friar Fuck".

The name sticks, even after she discovers he's celibate (because, *he's a priest*). Not letting that be any sort of deterrent, she spends the afternoon masturbating over him (but we really, really didn't need to see or even know this did we?) and visits the church to offer him some cans of food and her body. He again refuses her and can't get away from her fast enough. I would have run away too; Samantha at her most desperate is alarming.

Charlotte turns up at Trey's place much like the way he dropped in on her to end the last season: don't these people have phones? Charlotte has a written list of things she'd like to have a serious discussion about with Trey, such as their sex life. Trey doesn't want to talk about it, but the mere mention of it gives him a boner which he rudely takes out and comes on Charlotte's skirt within seconds. So very high school. Charlotte is appalled, but at least he offers to pay the dry cleaning bill.

The episode ends with a discussion about soul mates, which is kind of the underlying theme of the week: what are they, who believes in them, how many do you get. Opinions are plentiful, but I think we can all agree that Charlotte would be the furthest off the mark by asserting that in a world of billions of people, you only get one soul mate. I kind of wanted to pull up a chair at the table during this last scene and become the 5th SATC girl just so I could tell them all that soul mates are just something that freshly engaged and newlyweds like to call themselves before the reality of life sets in and they realise it's like unicorns when you're five years old: it's a cute idea but doesn't really hold still in reality.

2 "The Real Me"

Carrie appears in a fashion show with real models and it goes straight to her head (the phrase "pride before a fall" could have been coined about this episode). Miranda punches above her weight again and reacts differently this time (but still gets it wrong). Charlotte has never looked at her vagina in a mirror (oh come ON). Samantha gets a whole series of naked photographs taken and is dreadfully show-offy about it to absolutely everyone: the SATC girls, the photographer and team of assistants, the framer and the guy who delivers her fast food.

We discover that Charlotte has never checked out her vajayjay in a hand mirror, and I submit that she is the only western woman in the world who has never done this. Can she really be that prudish? Even the guy who painted her cunt has seen more of it than she has. In any case, her vagina is causing her some issues she won't discuss in company, and a doctor prescribes her an anti-depressant *for her vagina*. I've never heard anything quite so stupid – it's like when Samantha took Viagra to puff up her imaginary penis. It just appals me that members of the medical profession would be portrayed to do these kinds of things. Real doctors everywhere must be laughing at this plot line, or crying.

Miranda is picked up in her sweaty gym gear (and boy, does she sweat) by a guy who calls her sexy. The last time this happened, Miranda got horribly drunk and scared the guy off after he wrote her a note recommending she join AA ASAP. This time, Miranda decides to play up her alleged sexiness by becoming a different person: a bragging, vain, posing diva who's so off-putting the guy shrinks from her and later tells her she seems kind of up herself. Why doesn't Miranda just be herself for a change? She's has so much dating experience. SO much. She won't learn from her experiences and it pains me so. Of all the SATC girls, she's the one I'd spend time with over the other three, but then she ruins it by getting all poncey.

Charlotte is thrilled to attempt to match up two gay men Stanford and Anthony, but didn't count on Anthony, the biggest bitch on SATC, behaving so badly to the lovely Stanford that the proposed match turns out to be all kinds of awkward. I hope Anthony makes it up to Stanford later when they (spoiler alert) get married in the second SATC movie.

Carrie is hunted down by a pushy woman called Lynn who wants Carrie to be in her fashion show charity thing. At first, Carrie is mortified at the thought, but is eventually persuaded to appear as one of the "non-models" alongside the real models on the runway. Initially told she'd be wearing a spangly blue dress, Carrie is horrified when she is swapped for a pair of glittery undies. There's a bra and coat to go with it, so it's not that big a deal, but Carrie freaks out in her usual fashion, telling the producer she can't possibly wear those. I don't know. I've seen Carrie wearing less than this on the street. What about the last episode of last season, where she walked home in Big's shirt with a belt around it? Nothing says walk of shame more than that.

In any case, the undies and coat combo manage to look quite respectable, given that runways sometimes have a fair bit of transparency and bare skin. It's the shoes that are the problem: Carrie chooses the highest heels possible, not thinking about whether she'd be able to strut in them, and falls literally flat on her front in an excruciatingly embarrassing moment that I would never forget, especially after Heidi Klum steps over Carrie's sprawl like she was dog poo. Terrible, but also totes hilarious.

Style Note: I vote Carrie's non-model bouffant hairdo the second worst in the entire series. It's so bad it's not even good.

3 "Defining Moments"

Samantha decides to give lesbianism a shot, and doesn't spare us any details. Carrie is on a non-date with Big and gets picked up by a sax player right in front of Big (who doesn't like that one bit, boom!) Trey and Charlotte continue to have sex but the only thing that seems to excite Trey now is doing it in public places. There are so many facets to Trey's sexual problems, it's hard to keep track. Miranda is disgusted when her date has a cavalier attitude about sharing the bathroom.

Carrie spends a lot of time pondering over what it is that defines a relationship. This is because she is going out with Big now as though he is just a friend; a friend who tries to sabotage the intentions of any other man who is interested in Carrie. So I would define her relationship with Big now as a conflict of interest, with some unresolved issues from the past – somewhere just below friends with benefits, but above disinterested exes. There you go Carrie, put that in your column.

Miranda is offended when her latest man pees in front of her in the bathroom. I don't understand why this is a problem. He's not peeing *on* her. It's a normal bodily function that happens whether we like it or not and there's nothing to be embarrassed about. After all, they did far more obscene things the night before (I'm guessing). My point is, when you've seen each other's junk up close, is there much more to be embarrassed about? Once you're living together, these things are unavoidable – you're going to see your partner doing gross things unless you live in a palace with your own suite, so logically it's not a big deal.

Samantha for some reason heads into a full lesbian relationship with a temperamental artist and this raises a huge question for me. Why, when Samantha spends a lot of effort avoiding relationships with men that last longer than a night, sometimes literally pushing them away from her once they've popped their fizz, does she toss her convictions aside and launch into a settled partnership? Especially one where her new female lover is horribly jealous of any man Samantha has slept with (which means she's jealous anytime they go out in public)? It was never going to last, and thank goodness for that because the female ejaculation scene in the next episode is too gross for words, and before anyone calls me out for being sexist I'd just like to say that if it were a male orgasm it would never have been shown that graphically on an M rated TV series, so how it escaped censorship I'll never know. But that's in the future, because for now Samantha is holding off on having sex because she's pretending like she cares about whether this relationship will last or not, so for the first time in her life doesn't have sex on the first date. Yeeeeeaaaah.

Meanwhile, Trey is hot for Charlotte all over the city except at home: in cabs, movie theatres, restaurant bathrooms and appallingly, on the bed of the host at a party. I'm a bit disgusted with them both about that last one. Have they no shame? As for giving each other hickeys; Trey, this is right up there with coming on someone's skirt. Make it stop.

4 "What's Sex Got to Do with It?"

Miranda binge eats, to replace sex as she's in a dry spell. Samantha confirms her official lesbian status with graphic detail and it's TMI for me. Carrie has the best orgasm she's ever had with her jazz musician, but sadly a long-term relationship is not meant to be. Trey has turned into a sex maniac, so while Charlotte did get what she wished for, she's still not happy.

I was incredulous when Samantha announces to the girls that due to her recent foray into Maria's vagina, she has discovered that women have "three holes down there". This is something she should have known way, way before now, like from 36 years ago. It's basic female anatomy: did she think she wees out of her uterus? Also, as master of masturbation, how could she have been so ignorant on how to arouse a woman? It takes only minutes into their first lesbian lovemaking for Maria to tell her Samantha she has no idea what she's doing. I'm beginning to suspect that Samantha is actually a man in a blond wig. It would answer a lot of questions.

Miranda starts to eat chocolate cake and quickly develops a binge habit. She makes herself a whole cake, then begins to eat it piece by piece. She becomes so ashamed of herself that she pours dishwashing soap all over the last half of it as it sits in the bin. A waste of cake *and* soap; she could have just maybe given it to someone else or maybe developed a bit of self control and put it in the freezer for the next time she's in a dry spell.

Charlotte is becoming a bit sick of Trey's newfound confidence in his penis. At first it was all fun and games, having Trey make up for lost time with a vengeance as he jumped on her all over the city. But now he's just taking things too far with his talk of Charlotte measuring his hard-on with a ruler (something he should be able to do himself, and something he should have done in high school) and reminding Charlotte how hard his penis can get now. It's hard to believe that Trey could be any more boring, but there you have it. Even Charlotte is bored, and loses patience with him, telling him it's time to grow up and consider whether they are going to move back together and continue their farce of a marriage, or whatever. Trey pretends to think about it. I just yawned.

Carrie is also trying to make a relationship out of limited resources. The jazz player she is sleeping with may be able to give her glorious orgasms, but his mind is fixated on just jazz and nothing else. It's probably better than being fixated on his penis, but only just. Carrie decides to let this one go as well. It's a good idea, seeing as she hates jazz.

Best Quote: "She's just doing it to bug us". Charlotte, about Samantha becoming a lesbian.

5 "Ghost Town"

Aiden's back! I wonder what will happen? He and Steve, who seems like a strange choice for a business partner, open a bar together. Apparently, Miranda believes in ghosts. Charlotte moves back into Trey's apartment and immediately sets about spending huge amounts of his money redecorating it to their (her) taste. Samantha and Maria break up, thank goodness.

So Steve and Aiden open a bar together. This is rather a huge event, although somewhat downplayed by the SATC writers. Almost all small businesses fail, and although Aiden has experience making and selling furniture, it's not clear what experience he's had in the hospitality industry. Steve on the other hand can pull a beer, but can he write a business plan? Aiden is allegedly the "silent partner" in the process, so what makes him think Steve will be able to manage a workforce and the legalities and financials and all the other complex facets of a business? Miranda has previously commented that Steve isn't even an actor trying to be a barman; he's just a barman with no further ambition. I think the bar is a mistake for both of them. Anyway, I digress.

Carrie brings a pot plant for the new bar, as Steve has invited her to the opening (an invitation she thought was from Aiden). The bar opens, a party is thrown, and the rest is history. If history means: it's never seen again in the series, and only mentioned once or twice. What happened to it? All that capital expenditure! All that fit-out, some of which was hand made by Aiden! What an effort, to be lost at the end of the episode.

Carrie, Miranda and Samantha decide to attend the bar's opening (they have to, because it doesn't exist after this episode) after some deep consideration as to whether Carrie and Miranda can both be big girls and face their ex-boyfriends. It is at the bar where Carrie lets Aiden feed her a piece of celebration cake and she decides she still has feelings for him, ack! More on this next episode.

Samantha has a huge fight with Maria, to do with lots of things like their general incompatibility in all areas and Maria's uncontrollable jealousy about Samantha's men, who hover around her making sexy talk in front of Maria (well, they weren't to know Samantha was a lesbian now, were they? We can't blame them.) Maria smashes several of Samantha's dishes during their last fight, which is unforgiveable in my eyes; Samantha will be stepping on shards of crockery for months to come after that. They celebrate their breakup with a strap-on from Maria, which they give a thorough workout before parting ways. Which I really don't want to think about.

Miranda hears some creaking overhead at night time and decides it must be a ghost. It could just be the building creaking. I'm going with that.

Charlotte finds that now she has moved back in with Trey, her mother in law Bunny decides to make her presence felt at every opportunity, reminding Charlotte that just because Trey has taken her back, it doesn't mean Charlotte is the boss of Trey. Bunny decides which bed they will buy, suddenly turning up at the furniture store like she knew there was bed-shopping about to be done. She's also there the next day when Trey develops a chest cold, announcing that she's going to stay the night to look after him properly. It's almost as though Trey tells his mother everything that's going on so she can be involved completely, so he's not just boring but a mummy's boy too. Just you wait, Charlotte. There's so much more to come.

6 "Baby, Talk Is Cheap"

Carrie pesters Aiden into getting back together. Miranda has her butthole licked but isn't keen on returning the favour. Charlotte and Trey continue to have nothing to talk about, so they decide to have a baby: cue endless robot sex with little regard for ovulation cycles. Samantha gets ahold of the latest thing; a pair of fake nipples which she uses to attract a man who likes to baby-talk.

I can hardly watch as Miranda's marathon guy sticks his bum up in the air so high it practically touches the ceiling. Miranda seems to have similar trouble, partly because she knows what he means for her to do when he's doing that. I'm glad this is one of those sexual perversions that SATC only touches on once, because that's enough.

Charlotte's redecorating of Trey's apartment is in full swing, and together they decide to allocate one of the rooms as a nursery before they've even tried to get pregnant. Allocation is one thing, but actually going ahead and doing the renovation before said pregnancy is established is just a recipe for disaster (kind-of spoiler alert). They proceed to have awful sex where Charlotte actually discusses dinner plans while jumping around on top of him, and then Charlotte starts shopping for baby clothes while Trey has a silver rattle engraved (it may have been from Tiffany's). In the middle of all this jumping the gun, they host a dinner party for a couple and their three awful kids, which totally turns them off having sex for a whole week. After they decide that they'll probably only have one kid, and that their kid won't be a brat, they have sex again. See? No regard for timing. If it's not the right time of the month for Charlotte, there isn't any point having all that forced sex.

As I mentioned in last episode, Carrie decides she wants Aiden again, after she sees him with a new haircut at the opening of his new bar. He resists quite strongly, including yelling expletives at Carrie on his doorstep which must have woken the neighbours, which tells me he's not really that interested and she should have left it alone. But at the end of the episode they wind up having sex, which forces Aiden to reconsider the relationship and incredibly, decide to give it another go. I'm not sure it's such a good idea, Aiden. You are full of doubts and never really got over that whole being cheated on thing from last season. Also, Carrie is as selfish as ever, even asking Miranda to whisk Steve away from their group date before Miranda has had dessert – and we all know how much Miranda likes dessert – so that Carrie can be alone with Aiden to put the pressure on him further. It doesn't have the

111

markings of a great start to a second time around, but it'll provide some drama for this season I guess.

Samantha finally discovers something she doesn't like in bed – so there is something after all – it's baby talk from her newest hot man. He calls her breasts titty-witties, which I have to agree is pretty dreadful. Additionally, he's too immature to take her gentle feedback and that's the last we see of him. Between him and the butt-licker, that's two guys I'm ready to forget.

Questionable Plot Point: Carrie tells Aiden firmly that she's quit smoking, then takes a pack of cigs out of her bag then and there, throwing them onto the street. This in no way convinced me that she had indeed given up smoking, nor that she has any regard for the cleanliness of city streets.

7 "Time and Punishment"

Big causes a crapload of trouble for Carrie when he leaves one of his "hey baby" messages on her machine while Aiden is inside her. Miranda has a phone fight with Charlotte which results in Miranda somehow igniting a marathon injury and rendering her neck locked in one position. Samantha has sex with a guy she has literally known for five minutes after he steals her cab. He insults her and is thusly evicted from SATC at the end of the episode.

A lot of bad stuff goes on between Carrie and Aiden this episode; I'm making the call here that the phone message from Big which interrupts their game of hide the sausage is the catalyst for the (spoiler) eventual decaying of the relationship. Aiden is so jealous when he hears Big's voice that he sets out to even the score with Carrie by showing a lot of interest in a pretty girl at Scout (aha! There's a rare mention of that bar Aiden opened with Steve). Carrie falls over herself praising Aiden for helping a naked Miranda out of her cricked neck debacle when Carrie is too busy to help (and Carrie should have asked Samantha, or Charlotte. You know, one of Miranda's other friends). She also makes it clear to Aiden that she's practically perfect now for quitting smoking, but he isn't buying it and slaps her pretty hard when applying a nicotine patch to her back (I don't know why Carrie couldn't manage her patches herself and quit her disgusting habit without relying on Aiden to be a part of it. How hard is it to stick a patch on some skin you can reach yourself?)

Anyway, the upshot of all the drama is that Carrie refuses to cut Big out of her life entirely, because she "can't", even for Aiden, and he partially accepts this and goes back to cuddling her in bed in the mornings. For some reason Carrie thinks they are now in a "more honest place", but I'd call it a "more tenuous place" myself.

Charlotte has decided to quit work, encouraged by Trey. Hell, yeah! I know SATC is supposed to be about independent women not needing men, but seeing as we stray from this theme almost every episode, I have no problem with Charlotte becoming the person she was born to be: a stay-at-home housewife, cooking, cleaning, washing and attending her husband's engagements. There is no better SATC girl to fit this description, but the other three aren't having it. Instead of being happy for Charlotte for having it all, they warn her about her likely loss of identity and criticise her for doing what her husband wants. All three of them are in on this, but Charlotte chooses Miranda to target with her anger at being ridiculed, even though Miranda was possibly the gentlest in her critique of this life-changing decision. Charlotte calls up Miranda early in the morning to give her a serve and it ends with Miranda turning her head too fast and ending up lying on her bathroom floor, waiting for Aiden to turn up and do what Carrie was supposed to do. It's all forgotten by next episode, so don't worry. We never again have to hear condescension from Charlotte's friends about her early retirement. Nor do we ever hear an apology forthcoming from Charlotte to Miranda for being so needy as to demand Miranda's approval at 8:15am.

Although in replacing herself at the gallery, Charlotte interviews a load of young female wannabe art gallery managers but offers the job to pretty much the first one who walks in, without considering others or even sleeping on the decision. It's a strange way to hire new staff, so I hope it worked out for the gallery.

Samantha fights over a cab and ends up taking her opponent to her place so quickly it breaks a record even for her. The guy's a total tool, complaining over a few pubic hairs. (Remember when everyone had them?) It's hard to believe someone could be so fussy about such a small thing. But Samantha, never one to be picky, tells him he needs to lose all his if he's going to be such a fusspot. And so she performs possibly the first ever television manscaping, starting a trend of huge proportions perhaps because it gives men the idea it makes their penises look bigger.

8 "My Motherboard, My Self"

Aiden irritates Carrie when her laptop breaks by attempting to fix it in that special testosterone-filled way where he doesn't have a clue what he's doing but insists on trying anyway. Charlotte takes control of Miranda's mother's funeral, so I guess the Miranda/Charlotte altercation from last episode is well and truly put aside. Samantha suddenly can't orgasm.

Not only is Charlotte amazing at organising funerals, she also makes a damn good sandwich for the girls when they meet for lunch in the park (which seems like a great idea. All those café lunches must be horrendously expensive). It seems Charlotte is putting her retirement to some very good use, so nah nah nee nah nah SATC girls.

I can't help but wonder, though. Why are the SATC girls so damn rude to shop assistants? Charlotte snaps at the flower shop employee most unnecessarily, hissing at her that there must be "no crap" in the flower arrangement. It's not the first time we've seen such bad manners, and it's particularly galling from Charlotte who considers herself of fine breeding and refinement.

Miranda's mother dies, which is the most serious thing to happen to an SATC girl to date and it's terrific to hear that one of them even has a mother. Charlotte takes on the task of dealing with the flowers for the funeral as well as a gift for Miranda. Samantha, meanwhile, can't concentrate on the sadness of Miranda's situation and doesn't even bother to call her. She's got bigger things to worry about: after hours of sex and then masturbating, she can't reach a finale and expects her friends to be even vaguely interested or even sympathetic. Naturally they are instead appalled, and rightly so: this is a new level of self-absorbedness, even for SATC. No one slaps Samantha and tells her to snap out of it, so the search for her orgasm continues for pretty much the whole episode. I can help with one thing though: during the alleged sex scene with her new wrestling companion, the two of them go at it while wearing tight fitting lycra body suits. How the hell are they getting their uglies together with those leotards in the way? Might have been more effective to remove them, no?

Carrie is busy writing her column with Aiden at her apartment, and somehow manages to crash her Mac while attempting to discourage his interest in her prose. It's a spectacular crash complete with a sad face Mac, and after a visit to the Mac hospital we discover that Carrie never backs up her life's work on a hard drive so it's all lost forever (I wonder how they managed to create a book from her columns when they were all turned into gobbledegook?) Aiden is both irritating but then helpful, buying Carrie a new computer and backup system while Carrie lamely argues that she needs neither because her old system works fine. Aiden is furious at being shunted aside by Carrie's unwillingness to change her bad habits (again). Eventually contrite, Carrie apologises in her weird and wonderful way, telling Aiden she was too afraid to rely on him in case she ends up being too dependent and then they break up and she won't know how to do anything any more. The lack of logic here is typical for Carrie – she could have instead chosen to take advice and learn from others, to avoid making the same mistakes. Maybe one day.

Wardrobe Note: I know these days anything goes with style when attending a funeral, but did there have to be so much boobage on display at Miranda's mother's funeral from both Samantha and Carrie? It's quite distracting.

Annoying Plot Point: Samantha trying so hard to masturbate to orgasm that even she is bored of it. Doesn't she have any other hobbies? Might she consider quilting, crotchet or pottery, for example? What about the joys of reading a good book or taking a walk? The possibilities are endless. She doesn't even seem to own a damn television.

9 "Sex and the Country"

It's SATC's first brush with cancer, as Steve is diagnosed with it and turns to Miranda for support (possibly not the best choice, as she makes him cry about it). Charlotte and Trey continue their frenetic baby-making. Carrie feels duty bound to visit Aiden's holiday house for a weekend, but finds it not exactly to her standards. Samantha announces that weekends are for meeting new guys, so she doesn't have to keep fucking the old ones, reaching a new level of vulgarity. And just when I thought she couldn't go any lower.

I must say, I am impressed with Aiden's bottomless pit of financial security. There he is, announcing he has a holiday house in Suffern, as well as being able to buy Carrie's apartment and the one next door, and presumably somewhere else that he lives although that's not ever revealed. He has a largeish looking warehouse where he makes his wooden furniture. And let's not forget Scout, his business venture with Steve, because the writers of SATC seem to have. Carrie should have been taking a few notes from Aiden about financial security while she had the chance.

Aiden invites Carrie to see said holiday house in Suffern; then he insists that she visit after she tries to get out of it. Instead of packing for a country weekend away, Carrie dresses in a copy vintage 50s dress and stilettos, which is barely appropriate for a New York street let alone a cabin in the wilderness. When I go away, I like to have some sensible clothes to travel in, such as runners, cotton jersey tops and jeans. Clearly Carrie has no concept of this even though she has seen actual pictures of the shack she is about to weekend in. She is dismayed upon arrival and Aiden leaves her to survey the rusticness of it all while he does something around the back of the house. And there she spies a squirrel sitting harmlessly on the windowsill and overreacts in a major way with a high-pitched scream and hysteria that was totally unnecessary. Hasn't anyone living in New York who's visited Central Park seen quite a few squirrels in their lifetime? I visited New York once and even I saw a few of them. Later in the episode it scares her again, inciting another identical overreaction even though she's already been introduced to it. Aiden deserves a medal for not completely losing his cool at her ridiculousness. I mean for goodness sakes.

In the middle of the Suffern weekend away, Carrie travels back to New York allegedly to have a meeting with someone regarding her career but actually has dinner with Big as well/instead. I can't help but wonder if Aiden knew about this. Big is smitten with a famous actress and begins to tell Carrie about their sexual encounter, displaying total insensitivity and lack of discretion. It's an important scene though, because it contributes to the next episode's plotline. Fortunately Carrie stops him and we are spared too much detail.

Somehow, Carrie manages to persuade Samantha to visit the cabin with her when she returns after ~~her Big dinner~~ her important meeting regarding her career. Samantha, dressed every bit as inappropriately as Carrie for a weekend of roughing it, is even more unimpressed than Carrie with the ambience and lack of air-conditioning, making her disapproval felt in front of Aiden and not giving a shit if he hears. So not only does Aiden have his whining girlfriend there now, but also her whining friend. Luckily Samantha spies an eligible farmer within spitting distance and goes over there ~~for a fuck~~ to collect some milk from his cows. That keeps her out of everyone's hair for a while (except for the farmer's, ha).

Steve is diagnosed with cancer and chats to Miranda about it, where he displays a lack of knowledge about the disease in general and his diagnosis in particular. But he's in good hands with Miranda, who scares the shit out of him by telling him he could die and insisting he visit a proper doctor because according to her, his existing doctor is hopeless. I'm intrigued as to how many guys she discusses testicular cancer with at work - it seems a reasonable number of them have had the same thing (is it really that common amongst lawyers?)

Charlotte and Trey finally start paying attention to ovulation cycles and having sex when it's more likely to be effective instead of just hoping for the best at random times. This means they end up in Bunny's orchid hothouse at ovulation time, knocking over potplants while they attempt to inseminate. It looks both uncomfortable, dirty and also possible to get caught. But then Bunny has just watched her adult son taking a bath, so I suppose anything goes.

10 "Belles of the Balls"

Last episode we had Samantha taking up space at Aiden's country shack; this episode, it's Big. Aiden must be wondering who's next. The writers of SATC are getting a lot of mileage out this cabin lately. Samantha decides to approach Richard Wright (afore mentioned as Smarmy Richard) to nab him as her next big client. Steve is minus one ball and feeling down about it. Charlotte tries to suggest sperm testing to Trey in order to rule out one of the possibilities as to why they aren't pregnant after three whole months. Miranda gives Steve a mercy fuck, with long lasting implications.

Steve wants to investigate getting a prosthetic ball to fill up the loose skin in his scrotum. Miranda tries to talk him out of it, telling him it's just vain and unnecessary. To be honest I don't think it's such a terrible idea. Plastic surgery was very common even back in the 90s, and if it makes Steve feel like a man again, why not? As usual Miranda bosses him about asserting she knows best, ignoring the fact that even though Steve is a little … immature … he does have feelings and insecurities just like she does.

So Steve and Miranda get to discuss what size prosthetic testicle he should get, with him suggesting he'd suit a large and her supportively agreeing even though she's not really sure, in front of the doctor who at no point intervenes to explain to them that the size would be determined after measurement of the existing testicle. At least that's how I think it would work. Um…. doctor? Doctor?

In any case Miranda manages to talk Steve out of getting a silicon ball and gives him a mercy fuck instead, which they'll both regret in due course.

Speaking of balls, Charlotte asks Trey to get his tested for sperm quality and instead of acquiescing with this reasonable request (we know he can jerk off, we've seen it) he gets all petulant and storms off from the dinner table. This man is such a fussbudget. Charlotte is able to coax him into a sperm testing clinic where he is able to prove, with the help of some ball pulling by Charlotte, that his sperm is strong and manly (unlike Trey).

Big dares to track down Carrie at Aiden's shack (because she left her whereabouts on her answering machine, even though she's only away for a weekend and surely can just check calls from Suffern?) Big is so devastated by being dumped by his famous actress that he insists he must see Carrie immediately and talks her into having him visit her at Aiden's shack. Do these two have no idea, or shame? Carrie tries to pass Big off to Aiden as ~~her future husband~~ just a really needy friend, but Aiden is still displeased.

Poor Aiden, who has no say in this no say in it at all, has to come face to face with his nemesis who he can't stand, and watch Big drain all the alcohol in the joint without having the class to have brought his own. Big mutters incoherently, talking neither to Aiden nor Carrie, which makes me wonder why he couldn't have just done that at home. Eventually, after a sleepover and hangover, the two men slug it out by fighting in the mud, while a disgusted Carrie looks on, and then Aiden listens sympathetically to Big's woes over and over while a disgusted Carrie looks on. It was really "Big" of Aiden to put up with all this crapola.

Smarmy Richard initially refuses to offer Samantha the position as his publicist because he doesn't care for her active sex life, which is ironic because he's every bit as bad so he's really in no position to judge. Judge he does, and Samantha is hurt enough over this to cry in the lift on the way out of the building. She surprises me: I thought Samantha cared not a whit about being judged. Another surprise: Richard is endeared by her outburst in his office, right before she cried, and that alone is enough to make him change his mind and hire her anyway. Let's get this straight: Richard doesn't like the fact that she's had sex with every man in a one hundred mile radius, but she makes it OK by yelling at him that he's short sighted. Ah. Ok.

Questionable Plot Point: Big is confused that Carrie is in the country on a Thursday. Does he know that she doesn't work a 9 to 5 job and that she can pretty much write her weekly column wherever she happens to be and email it to her employer?

11 "Coulda, Woulda, Shoulda"

In SATC's most unfortunate of coincidences, Miranda finds out that Steve's single ball has made her pregnant, while a desperate Charlotte discovers her fertility is almost non-existent. Carrie revisits an abortion she had a while back. Samantha gains and loses a hot new client all in one episode.

Miranda's one egg producing ovary and Steve's lone nut have produced a pregnancy, and Charlotte is furious that it isn't hers. She's even more livid when she discovers that Miranda is going to terminate it, and the SATC girls minus Charlotte discuss their abortion histories. (We can safely assume in Charlotte's absence that she has never had one). Miranda's next dilemma is whether to tell Steve or not, and Carrie edges towards the belief that she should do so although a valid point is raised when Miranda points out that Carrie did not advise her inseminator 13 years ago.

We are taken to Saloon, the café where Carrie met the waiter she had sex with thirteen years ago, resulting in her pregnancy and abortion. Carrie struts in, chooses a table and is surprised (but not quite surprised enough) to see the very same waiter, from thirteen years ago, still waiting the same tables. I would describe this waiter as having a vast lack of ambition. Anyway, Carrie says hi to him like she expects him to remember her, and is a bit disappointed when he doesn't. He doesn't even so much as smile at her as he takes her order (he's a bit vacant behind the eyes if you ask me, but working the same tables for thirteen plus years will do that to a guy I suppose). Carrie orders a meal and then gets up from the table, drops some cash on it and leaves. I don't understand this. Was she hungry or not? She's not rich enough to behave like that.

Carrie accompanies Miranda to the doctor's office for her procedure. They have a discussion about whether it hurts, and how long it takes to feel "normal" again. Carrie forlornly assures Miranda that she'll be feeling normal "any day now", as if she's given her abortion even a second thought over the last 13 years.

Charlotte has completed a round of fertility testing, and she waits with Trey to receive the news. A doctor walks in having only half read the results, telling Charlotte that all is well, but then interrupts herself to announce with unbearable flippancy "Nope – spoke too soon!" like she thought she saw the bus coming but didn't. She tells Charlotte that her blood and mucus contain a bunch of anti-sperm troops, and throws in her random guess of a 15% chance of conception. How she arrives at this figure is undetermined, and probably negligently given – doctors shouldn't be giving out statistical estimates like this when they really have no idea. Has she had 1000 patients with this condition, and 150 of them got pregnant? Didn't think so.

Lucy Liu (yay – she's awesome) shows up as Samantha's new client, and Samantha wastes no time in using Lucy's name to get herself to the top of the Birkin bag waitlist, because there's no need for Samantha to justify a $4,000 bag. Samantha is shockingly rude to the Hermes rep over the phone, flinging Lucy's name around with a few expletives as she demands the bag arrive soonest (another example of an SATC girl being unnecessarily rude to the service industry). But it all backfires spectacularly when the bag is delivered to Lucy instead of Samantha and Lucy decides to keep it. Wave bye-bye to your $4,000, Samantha, as well as Lucy Liu, who heard about your bad manners from the Hermes rep. Ouch.

Carrie tells Aiden about Miranda's pregnancy but makes him swear to keep it from Steve, which is a breach of Miranda's trust as well as an imposition on Aiden. She then lies to Aiden about having an abortion. Boom! A trifecta of indiscretions.

In the end, Miranda keeps the baby, and Charlotte is gracious enough to congratulate her. The girls are having a baby.

Best quote: "Blah blah blah?" Lucy Liu mimics Samantha while discussing the free Birkin.

12 "Just Say Yes"

Miranda confesses to Steve that she's pregnant with his baby. Aiden proposes to Carrie, after deciding that he will buy her apartment and the one next door so they can live together. Samantha has sex with Richard Wright, the man who judged her sexual history and initially refused to hire her because of it. Charlotte continues to battle with Trey and his mother.

Trey is annoyed that Charlotte has researched their foray into IVF by discussing it with a few women in their building, but he's far worse because he tells absolutely bloody everything to his mummy, so he's in no position to complain. Bunny knows all about Charlotte's backup plan to adopt a Mandarin baby if their IVF is unsuccessful, and makes it known to Charlotte how displeased she is of this plan. Meantime, Trey is forced to inject Charlotte with hormones every night, which is nonsense because the hormones are usually injected into the stomach or thigh; places where a woman can actually reach herself. After all, they must be injected at exactly the same time each night, so it's somewhat unrealistic to need two people involved in this process.

Trey puts an end to the IVF anyway, by refusing to inject Charlotte and telling her he's changed his mind and can't be arsed continuing the fight to procreate, as well as tossing in for good measure that he's finding the whole marriage thing not to his liking. Didn't they have this conversation once before?

Carrie is horrified to discover that her building is going co-op. I had to look up what this means, because I'm not from New York. For the sake of plotlines in the next few episodes, it's worth pointing out that co-op buildings are blocks of apartments owned by a company, and the residents own shares in the company. The building is managed by a group of the resident "managers". Co-ops are very hard to get into – tenants are treated to a full personal and financial investigation, their applications to buy into the building subject to a very strict set of rules and the managers can refuse any application without even saying why. So Carrie is trouble here: she can't buy her unit outright, and her income and (lack of) assets would preclude her from getting a loan, as we will discover. Her finances probably aren't secure enough to qualify her as a renter of the new "owner", so she's out on her arse, a fact she discloses to Aiden (who doesn't understand why she just can't buy into the co-op. Does he know anything about her income, lifestyle and shoe addiction? Even we know more about all this than he seems to).

So instead, Aiden proposes that he buy her apartment, and the one next door, and knock down the wall between the two. It's a mad idea for several reasons, partly because of the high chance of this offer being knocked back well and truly by the corporation (holes in walls? I doubt that's allowed) and partly because at least one of the people in this relationship isn't really sure it's for life. But we'll get to that.

Samantha meets her new client Richard Wright, who busts her arse for screwing up the first assignment she was given, and then forgives her when she snaps at him about how she resolved it and assures him it won't happen again. Her lack of contriteness and defensiveness somehow appeals to Smarmy Richard, who seems to really like it when women have "balls", i.e. when they yell at him after he's ticked them off. They have a discussion about how marriage is for losers and sleeping around is much more fun. It's already the weirdest working relationship ever: I could not imagine having this sort of conversation on day one of my new job, especially after I'd managed to stuff something up. As Samantha doesn't care who she sleeps with and basically has no standards, she could have decided to not mix work with sex, in order to keep her client, income, reputation, etc intact. There are plenty of other non-client fish in the sea. But this is Samantha we're talking about here; you know what happens next.

Miranda tells Steve about the baby and he's ok with it. All good.

Carrie finds a fugly diamond ring in a box while she's snooping through Aiden's bag. She reacts by vomiting, mostly because she knows he's about to propose but also because the ring is hideous. It transpires that Miranda is responsible for this – she helped Aiden pick out the ring, which Charlotte and Samantha also think is heinous. But the ring is never actually presented to Carrie. When Aiden does finally get down on one knee, the ring he offers to Carrie is completely different. But I want to know how Aiden knew to get the ring changed. If he never gave it to Carrie, how did he know it was bad? Miranda denies all responsibility, telling Carrie she's "out of this now". Carrie accepts the proposal with the new ring, and immediately starts having doubts. This will make for some tense viewing over the next few episodes.

Meantime, Steve gets hold of the fugly ring Miranda chose, and offers it to her as a proposal. At least he got the ring right, but Miranda tells him to get stuffed. There's a girl who knows how to make a decision.

We cut to Samantha and Richard, dry humping in a private jet as they travel to Brazil to a property that he needs her to see. Too soon, so inappropriate. He even rips her clothing as they get it on in front of the co-pilot – I can't help but wonder if she will wear ripped clothes to her property viewing.

13 "The Good Fight"

Trey puts the final nail into the coffin that is his marriage. Charlotte hosts a dinner party for the girls, seeing as she threw away her career and has nothing else to do now that her baby-making days are over. Miranda has sex with a man not the father of her baby, after she's cleared it with Carrie first. Samantha and Smarmy Richard continue to fuck, and we see a frontal glimpse of his long, pink dick-a-licious penis.

Trey brings home a cardboard cut-out of a baby as a joke gift for Charlotte, making Charlotte horrified and heartbroken. It is a heartless thing for a man to do; especially as Trey is supposedly an educated, intelligent doctor. I hate to think of his bedside manners.

Aiden moves in with Carrie, which was so quick – I mean, he has to sell his place, obtain permission from the co-op to move in with his dog (pets are often forbidden in co-op buildings) and get the go ahead to knock a hole in the shared wall. Plus he would have had to undergo the scrutiny I mentioned in last episode's rundown, which entails just about everything but a prostate exam. All this takes many months in the real world. But here he is, filling Carrie's apartment with so many boxes it's impossible to even walk around the place. He could have maybe just put it all in storage, because once the renovation starts, everything will be covered in dust anyway. It's not like he's short of a quid.

He also brings a pot plant into the apartment, which Carrie moans about – it seems to offend her more than even the boxes, the dog, Aiden's demands on her wardrobe space and the general mess. I'd have thought the houseplant was the smallest of the issues. By the next week, it's dead. Did Aiden expect Carrie to look after it? Why didn't he water it, seeing as it was his plant?

The girls press Samantha for details about Smarmy Richard but for once she's not talking. Also, she's upset that Carrie has blabbed the news of her newest conquest to the other two. Carrie teases her about it, telling her that she must "like" him. So in order to lay that idea to rest, Samantha tells them all about his long, pink, amazing dick. Which pretty much shuts them all up on the subject, thank goodness. I'm sure they don't need to hear about the blow job Samantha gave him in his office, during working hours, under his desk, with floor to ceiling clear glass surrounding them.

Charlotte and Trey have an enormous fight at her girls' dinner which Charlotte warned Trey to steer clear of. Trey can't put a foot right any more, and appears during the meal to bring up the subject of the cardboard baby, resulting in a screaming match about flaccid penises (Trey's) and babies (cardboard ones). But it's the last Charlotte and Trey fight we'll have to watch.

Miranda has hot sex with a hot guy, after deciding it's worth the risk of "denting" the baby. She thinks it's the last chance she'll ever have at sex now that the baby is nearly due. But she needn't worry. This is SATC, after all.

14 "All That Glitters"

Extroverted Carrie is beginning to realise that she has begun to cohabit with an introvert. Charlotte organises to have her apartment photographed for House & Garden, but Trey moves out before the article is even published. The SATC girls visit a gay bar (why?) where

Miranda bumps into a co-worker who's been in the closet. Samantha takes drugs.

Seeing as Aiden won't go out to a new restaurant for dinner, Carrie goes out dancing with the SATC girls. Why they would choose a gay bar is curious. Aren't there about a million other places they could go for dancing? The gay bar has no female toilets (and this alone would be enough to make me want to leave the joint. If the manager is going to allow women in the premises, he could at least provide women's facilities. Hasn't he heard of lesbians?) It is in the bathroom that Samantha openly ogles all the penises on display, which in normal circumstances would be seen as perverse, creepy, socially unacceptable and would probably get her kicked out. I mean, imagine if a man did that at a lesbian bar. He'd be torn to shreds. Miranda, meanwhile, bumps into a colleague she didn't know was gay and confesses to him that she's pregnant, to make him feel better about the fact that he's hiding something at work. So it's entirely her own fault that he narcs on her and everyone at work finds out. Secret keeping is not a strong point within the SATC crowd.

And nor it seems is behaving sensibly, since Samantha has taken an ecstasy pill from some random at the bar. Sadly, Samantha, a grown woman who should know better, again risks her health and safety doing stupid things. She takes herself off to Smarmy Richard's for a fuck, seeing as she's heard that sex on X is incredible. Do let us all know, Samantha.

The girls gather at Carrie's to watch gay porn (again; why?) which only Charlotte is peeved about, as it's not really to her taste. They discuss the fact that Charlotte and Trey are now in separate bedrooms, and *House & Garden* is coming to photograph their perfect home and perfect marriage and it's all just pretence because Trey isn't even excited about it. But even if their marriage was going along swimmingly, why would he care about *House & Garden*? Before Charlotte came along, Trey was content to live amongst duck mallards and plaid. I would say he's never read a design magazine in his life.

After the photoshoot, where the couple sadly fake their happiness, Trey goes back to Bunny (makes sense). Charlotte sure is lucky it wasn't her who had to move out. They're a way away yet from settlement per the pre-nup.

Carrie has met an Australian guy at the gay bar, and by the way thanks to the writers for casting an actual Australian in the role of Oliver, hot gay shoe distributor. I'm yet to see a non-Australian actor make a convincing Australian accent; the closest I've seen is Robert Downey Jr in *Tropic Thunder*, who is so incredible in that movie I'll love him forever. But I digress. Carrie starts to hang out with Oliver, who quickly becomes her new BFF because he thinks Carrie is just fab and flatters her accordingly. So Carrie is pretty pissed off when Oliver takes her to an exclusive bar and Stanford steals him in front of her. Sensing the night will only get more shitty, Carrie heads home in a sulk to be with her homeboy Aiden, but things are beginning to crack there, too. Carrie can no longer bear to see her engagement ring on her finger, and has started wearing it around her neck on a chain. This is an extremely risky way to wear an expensive diamond; on a thin chain that can be caught and snapped, especially in crowded gay bars with exuberant gay men flinging their selves all over the dance floor. But you know, pretty soon wearing an engagement ring won't be a concern for Carrie anyway.

15 "Change of a Dress"

Carrie can hardly barely to think about her wedding, so Miranda hopes to get Carrie into the spirit of it by taking her dress shopping at a hideous wedding dress store. Charlotte isn't in the mood for solo tap dancing at tap lessons and has a meltdown when the instructor asks her to tap by herself for five seconds. Samantha thinks she's caught monogamy because she's developed feelings for Richard and it's a completely alien sensation for her. Miranda is about as excited by her pregnancy as Carrie is at being engaged.

Charlotte is filling her spare time with lots of different things, but it's not relaxing her or taking her mind off her broken marriage. Throwing yourself into a new, fun activity can distract you for a little while, to get away from life's troubles, but Charlotte's fragile state of mind goes into high gear when she is the last one standing during doubles tap dancing across the floor. She could have just concentrated on learning her steps, but instead makes a Carrie-esque spectacle of herself and chucks a tanty about the odd number of students in the class. I'm assuming she won't be showing her face there again.

Carrie continues to wear her diamond ring amongst the ghetto-trash jewellery around her neck, where she has to keep fishing it out of there on demand. She keeps forgetting she's engaged, and doesn't want to talk about it with old cast members like Susan-Sharon (I wondered what happened to her). Complaining to Miranda that she can't get excited about her wedding, Miranda is in the same boat because she's the only one who can't get excited about having a boy. Carrie lets Miranda talk her into going to a flouncy wedding dress boutique which couldn't possibly be anywhere near New York because the kind of dresses they sell might only be bought by brides in the Bible Belt of USA. They troop into the store and tell various and obvious lies to the shop owner, who is not fooled and resists the urge to tell them to fuck off out of there as they're clearly not genuine customers.

Hilarity ensues as the brides-to-be frock up in two relics of design from the 1980s, and cackle until they can hardly draw breath. But then something akin to terror overcomes Carrie, who flushes with a sudden fever and burning rash as she begs Miranda to rip the dress off her. Rip it off she does, buttons flying everywhere and lace shredding. Another cost Carrie can ill afford, especially when it winds up in a nearby dumpster bin after (I assume) someone actually paid for it. The shop owner must have been furious.

16 "Ring A Ding Ding"

Carrie finally faces 10 years of irresponsible money management by finding herself on the brink of losing her apartment after Aiden moves out and tells her she must buy the apartment from him. Charlotte clings to the remains of her tattered marriage, by wearing her engagement ring around the house. Miranda is pregnant and farting a lot. Samantha tries to trick Richard into telling her he loves her.

It's a wonder that Charlotte doesn't leave the series forever after the way Carrie treats her in this episode.

Imagine this: *your most airheaded friend is about to be kicked out of her apartment due to her financial "cul-de-sac" and everyone else stupidly offers to loan her the money to buy it. Knowing that she buys a pair of $400 shoes every other week, as well as having sole income from a weekly column of no more than 600 words, you stay quiet. You know full well that loaning more than $25 to this person would be a huge mistake, if you wanted much of it back.*

Later, your friend pops by your apartment to give you hell about your alleged meanness and accuse you of having mental issues because you are still wearing a beautiful piece of jewellery that your ex-husband gave you.

Not only did they make up, but Charlotte gives Carrie the expensive diamond ring, as loan for the down payment deposit – and then, get this – *it is never mentioned again*. Do you think Carrie ever paid that money back? Because in the very next episode she is wearing a new suit and

$200 haircut for her first meeting at *Vogue*. At least *Vogue* pays her $4.50 a word – but they hated her first column, so…..

There are just a few things I don't understand in this episode. For starters, couldn't Aiden have sold the apartment to another buyer with a long lease attached in Carrie's name? Surely there's someone in New York who would have been happy to make an investment like this? Or perhaps, seeing as Aiden went to all the trouble of buying into a co-op, he could have fixed the hole in the wall then simply become a landlord to adjoining apartments? As it is, only one of the apartments is sorted when Carrie buys it (explained below), so what happened to the other apartment that Aiden is still the owner of?

How was Carrie planning to finance the purchase of the apartment "all by herself", as she announces firmly after ripping up a cheque from Big, who happily provided her the down payment? Maybe she could have had sex with Gilles another 29 times.

If financing her apartment by herself was her plan, why did Carrie then accept Charlotte's engagement ring, especially after she had said to Charlotte (only a few days ago) that she would have turned any offer of a loan down? Why did the two of them have to go to a fancy restaurant to apologise to each other (even though Charlotte didn't do a thing wrong)?

How on earth does Carrie manage to repay not only a mortgage, but also Charlotte? How come Carrie doesn't know that 100 times 400 is 40,000?

Charlotte had a momentary lapse when she kissed goodbye to her $30,000 forever, but let's face it, she can afford it. She's living in an expensive apartment that she "earned" by being married to the boring but perfectly nice Trey for a little while, making sure there was a decent pre-nup. She may be complaining about having to volunteer instead of being paid because she's too "overqualified", but so what. She doesn't have to work, so she can just be the princess she is. Awesome for her.

Not a lot of other interesting stuff happens in this episode, but for completeness I'll tell you that Samantha has fallen in love with Smarmy Richard and tricks him into telling her he loves her too, drawing his personal assistant into the sneaky plan. Miranda draws Steve into her plans for management of the baby that hasn't even arrived yet, and they also have another mercy fuck.

Questionable Plot Point: Carrie's earning of $4.50 a word at Vogue. Something about this screamed bullshit to me, so I did a bit of research. After all, at $4.50 a word, Carrie could write a 500 word article (about a page and a half of this book) and earn $2,250. Not meaning to brag or anything, but I write a page in at most 20 minutes, 30 minutes max after I've edited and tightened it up a bit. So according to that pay rate, I'd be earning about $3,000 an hour, give or take. This seemed a bit unrealistic to me, compared to say, what you'd earn as a lawyer, accountant or doctor, even when we take Carrie's C-grade celebrity status into account. When I Googled it, the rates for freelance writers vary widely, but given that my research takes place about 17 years after season 4, you could earn anything from $100 to $700 for a 500 word article, or as little as $0.20 a word up to $1.50 if paid by the word. Backdate those numbers 17 years and I think you'll see where I'm coming from. Even if Vogue did offer $4.50 a word, which I think is unlikely, Carrie never had any articles published by them, that we know of, so it doesn't explain her $400 shoe habit and Manhattan apartment.

17 "A '*Vogue*' Idea"

Candice Bergen (yay!) shows up as Carrie's new boss lady at Vogue, and makes Carrie feel like crap about the quality of her first Vogue column. Samantha somehow manages to get a waitress half their age to have sex with her and Richard for Richard's birthday present. Charlotte goes beserk organising a baby shower for Miranda.

Carrie has a soul-destroying meeting at *Vogue*, where her new boss lady hates her work and has scribbled all over it in red pen. Has boss lady never read Carrie's column before? I'm not sure how she got the job, although it may have had something to do with the boss lady's assistant Julian, who later tries to get Carrie drunk in order to comfort her/boost her ego. Later in the episode, it appears Julian's main motive was to get Carrie in the sack, after he strips off in the *Vogue* wardrobe in an attempt to woo her (that was never a good plan, especially with those socks).

Right before that horrifying display, Carrie discovers a pair of Manolo Mary Janes at *Vogue*'s wardrobe, and makes a big fuss about squeezing her feet into them. How big are her feet? She's a 5'2" size 2 and she's somehow having to force her feet into a pair of heels that a model would normally wear - they are 5'10" plus, with feet several sizes larger than Carrie's, so why are those shoes too small?

It's back to threesomes once more as Samantha asks Richard what he'd like for his birthday and he requests a threesome with one of the most stunning women we'll see on SATC. Samantha pretends she's ok with this but her jealousy is palpable through the TV screen. She brags to Carrie that she has far more expertise than Alexa and will embarrass Alexa with her prowess. It already sounds like it's going to be a horrible afternoon for at least the women in this arrangement.

I can't help but wonder what Alexa, the blonde who must be no more than 21, is getting out of this. Why on earth would she be up for having sex with crusty Richard and Samantha, people more than twice her age? Nevertheless, the girl is "up for anything" and they all jump on the bed and start going at it. But part of the moves in Samantha's repertoire include shoving Alexa off the bed, not letting her get near Richard. Alexa implores Richard to put Samantha in her place by referring to him as "daddy", which was a big mistake, but a lucky one too, because Richard instructs Samantha to get rid of her and Alexa gets to dodge a bullet by leaving the three way. It's the best way, Alexa, trust me.

Charlotte is put in charge of Miranda's baby shower by a reluctant Miranda, who hates baby showers so much she can hardly bear the thought of her own. And instead of doing it subtle, Charlotte turns it into a wedding-style event, ignoring Miranda's menu requests and opting for a centrepiece on the table (which I didn't even know people did for anything outside of weddings). The two SATC girls end up fighting about it, and Miranda even threatens to boycott the whole thing, but it all ends well when Charlotte does include some fried chicken and there are lots of gifts. It still looks like a boring party though.

Carrie gets to keep her job at *Vogue*, although it's been a bad start. Her boss hates her work, Julian has sleazily come onto her in the *Vogue* wardrobe, and she's made a fool of herself by getting drunk and staggering through the office with half the staff seeing the spectacle. Nevertheless, she somehow manages to keep the job, which is lucky because she still has to pay Charlotte the $30,000 back. But just like the $30k, we never hear of *Vogue* again.

18 "I Heart NY"

Samantha is firmly in love with Richard and buys him a tacky gift as well as acting like a crazy jealous lady (which does nothing to endear her to Richard). Big moves away from NY and almost got away with it without Carrie finding out. Miranda pops out her sprog. Charlotte begins to date again now that Trey has gone forever, but finds the quality of the dating pool wanting.

Carrie randomly calls up Big and invites herself over to his apartment in the middle of the night, but is stunned to discover, in the usual unexpected way she discovers things about Big, that he has bought a vineyard and is moving to Napa. All this must have taken some planning, but Big hasn't thought to include telling Carrie as part of the planning process. Kudos to Carrie, she handles it well, but misses the opportunity to have a last roll in the hay, a decision she'll regret because it will be her last chance (this season, anyway).

Planning a last date with Big the next day, Carrie spies a hideous pair of designer pink frilly shoes that she must have in order to wear to this date. Given her financial situation and that Big will for sure not even notice them, it is ridiculous that she even considers buying them. But buy them she does. If I were her, I'd keep this a secret from Charlotte, who expected that her loan to Carrie would be a "clean and simple" transaction, meaning that repayments would be forthcoming. I think Carrie misunderstood the arrangement.

I don't know what it is about Smarmy Richard that Samantha likes so much (and I need to question at this point if he is still her client, because if he is, that's about to be blown out of the water), but when she discovers him going down on another pretty girl she is livid and heartbroken. It's a curious switch of attitude by Samantha, who up till now has spent a lot of time avoiding monogamy and poo-pooing the very notion of it, literally pushing away the men who thought they'd be getting a second go at her. She's always been immune to infidelity, not caring if her lovers were even single. Samantha smashes the cheap-looking awful framed picture she bought him (a picture of three red hearts in a frame) and Richard looks a bit relieved that he'll now never have to hang it.

Miranda gives birth to her baby, after she's interrupted Carrie's Big date and cockblocked Carrie who now no longer gets to give Big a goodbye romp. Miranda also breaks her waters all over Carrie's new pink shoes, ensuring that they were now a complete waste of money. Carrie makes her way back to Big's apartment after the birth, but Big has already left for Napa. I don't know why Carrie suddenly now has a key to Big's apartment after it was such a thing in prior episodes that he would never give her one. But Big has left Carrie a plane ticket in his apartment, in case she ever wants to visit him in Napa. Curiously, as far as we know, she never does.

10 Worst Dates on SATC

1. Carrie's dull phone-salesman fuck buddy, trying to sell her his wares over sushi
2. Miranda being lectured about freezing her eggs by a guy who has hair plugs
3. Carrie and Berger, all of them but especially the one where Charlotte crashes their date and is forced to endure their bickering
4. ...and the one where Carrie backpedals as fast as she can to Berger about her scrunchie remark, which he is so salty about that he can't even look at her
5. Charlotte trying to make conversation about summer camp with the one-track Mr Pussy
6. Carrie discovering that Big is engaged
7. Charlotte realising that her knight in shining armour was just a big bully looking for punch-ups
8. Carrie on her date with Harry's groomsman, the night before Harry and Charlotte's wedding, where she has awful sex and can't even stand up straight the next day
9. Aleksandr attempting to use Carrie's kitchen for cooking even though she has virtually no kitchenware, then killing a live mouse in said kitchen
10. That guy who slobbers all over Charlotte's face for a goodnight kiss

Season 5

1 "Anchors Away"

Carrie decides to date New York instead of men, seeing movies by herself and pretending to have no interest in hunky sailors during Fleet Week. Charlotte hasn't had sex since Trey, and is very keen to attend the navy party that a horny sailor has invited Carrie and any/all of her friends to. Samantha spreads the word about what an arsehole Richard is. Miranda feels left out of her old life now that she has Brady.

Miranda is a new mother, but somehow still manages to attend all the regular café meetings that the girls hold. In the real world, new mothers barely have enough time to shower, and yet Miranda doesn't miss so much as a cappuccino, albeit looking like crap. Why she'd want to drag her newborn around town instead of getting all the sleep she needs before she has to haul herself back into her job is a puzzle no new mother would ever understand. Additionally, she leaves baby Brady, who appears to be about 4 months old at this point, with Samantha of all people, who is about the last person to know anything about, or have a vague interest in, babies. This is because Miranda can't just adopt a mum bun like everyone else for a few months – I mean, she has a newborn, who cares what a new mother looks like - so instead she happily takes Samantha's place at the hair salon without giving so much as a 30 second training lesson in nappy changing. Brady starts crying pretty much on sight of Samantha – I would have, too.

It's Fleet Week, which means the city is full of sailors looking to have a ~~fuck~~ good time and picking up random women as they get into cabs (eg. Carrie). Despite having announced that she's having a glorious time being single, Carrie takes Samantha and Charlotte to a huge Navy party where Charlotte lets one sailor get a look at her boob (this was the girl who wouldn't bare a breast in a sauna full of women, but will show a random sailor in full view of others, including Carrie who gets an eyeful when she stumbles upon them). Carrie is so freaked out by seeing both Charlotte's and Miranda's (breastfeeding) boobs that day that she suggests that Samantha show hers as well. Never missing an opportunity to be an exhibitionist, Samantha flashes the whole entire party, to Carrie's shock. But we've seen them many times, so it wasn't that much of a shock to the rest of us.

Meanwhile, Miranda has a total freak-out over Brady's belly button scab, which falls off while she's changing his nappy and lands on the floor. The cat starts playing with it, and Miranda screams in horror. She calls Steve to help her "deal" with it.

This kind of worries me. Miranda may be yet to face a poo explosion, otherwise known as a number three, and if she finds a belly button scab so objectionable I have no idea how she's going to manage all the disgusting things that happen when you are looking after a baby. Also, Miranda has a cat. How is it possible that her cat hasn't primed her for this by doing all the disgusting things cats are known to do, such as: spit up furballs on the rug; throw up their entire dinner moments after eating it; catching and decapitating rodents and insects; and of course leaving their daily waste in a box which must be emptied manually by their owner, i.e. Miranda? Has Fatty the cat never done these things? He hasn't prepared Miranda for parenthood very well.

Samantha is being bombarded by calls from Richard who is desperate to have her back. Samantha embarks on a campaign to smear his bad name all over the city by handing out and pinning flyers to posts all over the neighbourhood with Richard's face labelled as a cheater and liar. She also pretends to meet him for a date but only goes to throw a perfectly good drink in his face. I really think this is taking things too far. He didn't do anything that she hasn't done in the past with other women's husbands – she's been very blasé about that thus far – so all this revenge carry-on just makes her look like a fruit-loop. It also makes her look like she cares about Richard. He may well be regretting he hired her in the first place, now that she's using her PR skills to advertise his flaws.

Amusing Plot Point: Carrie meeting her possible future self in a soup café, a crazy old single woman nattering about her lost loves, wearing clothes and a hairstyle decades too young for her and sprinkling lithium in her food.

2 "Unoriginal Sin"

Steve wants to get Brady baptized so the small, innocent child doesn't end up in hell. Carrie is fretting about being sacked from her one measly job (and whatever did happen to Vogue?) but instead it turns out she's about to become an author of a compendium of her own recycled columns. Charlotte is desperate to find her next great love so starts attending seminars held by one of those crackpots touting love advice (much like Carrie did in her "how to find love" series). Samantha actually takes Richard back, displeasing her fellow SATC girls.

In addition to wasting money on "believing in love" seminars, Charlotte also wastes lipstick by drawing affirmations on her mirror with it. I seriously don't know what is stupider than this. How are you supposed to do your makeup with graffiti written all over it? How annoying is it to remove half a lipstick tube from your mirror? And how does anyone believe that writing on a mirror will make things happen, like finding a man and being happy ever after?

Charlotte drags Carrie along to one of the seminars about positive affirmations held by some crooked doctor taking money off people to tell them that you can have anything you want just by wishing and wanting hard enough. Carrie sees straight through it, but Charlotte is taking it all very seriously. It is at the seminar that Charlotte discovers Carrie has been asked to be Brady's godmother, and even worse – Carrie seems to misunderstand the obligations of godparenthood, treating it as a bit of a lark. Charlotte thinks she could have done a much better job of it and is infuriated that Miranda didn't select her instead. But when you think about it, neither Steve nor Miranda especially are particularly religious, so there is little to zero chance that Charlotte would have ever been called upon to be of any assistance with official godparental duties. So there's no need for her to sit glowering at Carrie, when Carrie isn't the one to be cross at. Charlotte can be so petulant about the silliest of things (and yet, never asked Carrie for her $30,000 back).

Carrie, bless her, does implore Miranda to reconsider her choice of godparent, but she does it *at the christening* – way too late - her name's already on the program, so it's a done deal. To her credit, Charlotte does show an interest in the proceedings by taking photographs of the baby and his entourage, which was good of her. To be honest she surely would have been a better long-term choice than Carrie, even if the position was in name only.

Smarmy Richard has accompanied Samantha to the christening, because Samantha is keen to inflict as much punishment as she can on the man, including making him attend boring religious ceremonies. After the ceremony, Richard feels it necessary to approach Miranda to tell her that he "got scared". It's a mystery as to why he feels the urge to make this bizarre confession to Miranda, whom he barely knows. What was he scared of, though? Scared that he was developing feelings for Samantha? Scared he can't have sex with another woman again now that he's monogamous to Samantha, more like. In which case, he should stop telling Samantha he "loves" her and just call it quits. Richard is a hard man with little emotion, so he shouldn't have found that too difficult. Samantha's going to give him the easy way out soon enough.

We meet Steve's mother, a crazy outspoken woman who appears slightly drunken. Carrie dedicates her ~~compendium~~ book to Charlotte, as it's supposed to be a message of hope, and who is more hopeful than Charlotte? I hope it makes up for not being a godparent.

Miranda moment: Miranda telling Carrie that the baptism is "one less bath" she'll have to give Brady. I just know I'd get along with Miranda IRL.

Questionable Plot Point: Steve jumping the gun again by attaching a toilet safety device to the seat. The baby is approximately two months old and will be in no need of safety devices around the house until he's crawling, which could be anything from six to twelve months away. That toilet seat clip is going to drive Miranda crazy.

3 "Luck Be an Old Lady"

Carrie, for some reason, is hell bent on all the SATC girls celebrating Charlotte's 36th birthday, which isn't even a proper milestone birthday and Charlotte doesn't even want to acknowledge it. Samantha's jealousy about Richard ramps up a few notches. The girls head to Atlantic City for the party because Samantha was going there with Richard anyway.

Carrie presses the girls into taking up Richard's offer of a private jet ride to Atlantic City, so that they can have birthday dinner together there while Richard plays poker. Charlotte gets stuck on the jet with just Richard and Samantha when the other two SATC girls miss the flight due to a babysitting crisis. Richard and Samantha behave inexcusably – getting it on right in front of Charlotte, while she knits and wrinkles her nose in distaste. Well, so would have I - Richard and Samantha are (allegedly) grown adults who have access to private places to have sex any time of day or night, so why do it in front of Charlotte, who is known to be a bit prudish and not into voyeurism? It's just too icky for words.

Charlotte attends her girls' birthday dinner wearing a white high-necked ruffled shirt and her hair done like a 1960s Pan Am air hostess. She's worn sexier things to work. *(She's worn sexier things to do the laundry and cook dinner)*. I get that the idea is to contrast her against the "woman who lost all her money and has to turn tricks" outfit that she later wears (it's a piece of red spandex that she purchased at the casino store). But the contrast is so contrived it's kind of like a reverse makeover, where you take a hot girl and make her look really daggy for a few hours so you can make her look hot again with no effort. Charlotte does not normally dress like an uptight choirgirl, so it's out of character to see her like this at her own party.

The party ends up being a bust though, as Charlotte is too cranky to be happy about being 36, especially after Miranda buys her a pack of Old Maid cards and some guy at the casino refers to Carrie as "the hot one" in front of Charlotte. Samantha is too paranoid to leave Richard alone at the poker table with all the cheap hookers around the place (I really don't like Samantha much at all when she's in this Richard relationship. She's a needy, obsessed bore). Miranda crashes and heads off to bed early, so that's it: they've travelled all the way to Atlantic City to bicker, be insecure and go to bed early.

Samantha's jealousy reaches fever pitch. She is so sure that Richard's conference call in his hotel room is a cover for sex with one of the hotel maids that she runs all the way up the fire stairs to burst into Richard's hotel room in sureness that she will catch him between some woman's legs. She could have just waited for a lift, especially when she is wearing the pearl thong Richard gave her, which is so uncomfortable she must tear it off – in the fire stairs, mid-run. Well duh! Pearl thongs are a sex toy, aren't they? Correct me if I'm wrong, but people don't generally wear nipple clamps and dildoes to the casino to play roulette. I don't know why Samantha considers a pearl thong "day wear".

Samantha doesn't find Richard up to anything much, but still decides it's time for this tense, immature relationship to end. Thank goodness, because I'm tired of covering my eyes every time they go at it.

Carrie earns a $1,000 chip by blowing on a dice for the gambler who called her the "hot one", and instead of cashing it in immediately and using it to, I don't know, maybe pay Charlotte back a bit, she plays it on the roulette table. Of course she blows it. (Also, she's just coughed up shouting dinner for all the girls, including lobster.) In addition to knowing nothing about budgeting, clearly she also knows nothing about gambling: if she really *had* to spend that $1,000, it should have been on the black v white, where the odds are much better at 1:2. Miranda is horrified that Carrie gambled and lost, but earlier in the very same episode runs out of money herself and tells Carrie "we're going to need that chip" so she can continue to gamble. Contradictory much?

Miranda Quote: To Steve, about Brady: "But we made an agreement this week. Monday to Friday, I try not to kill him. Saturday and Sunday, you try not to kill him." Summing up parenthood perfectly. Miranda, you kill me.

4 "Cover Girl"

Charlotte goes to a bookstore to find self-help books on how to get over your past loves and find new ones, but is confronted with a series of desperate looking women reading the same books. Carrie and Samantha have differing ideas on what would be appropriate for the front cover of her ~~compendium~~ book. Miranda goes to Weight Watchers, probably still upset over the fat-shaming she received in the last episode at the casino. Carrie catches Samantha giving a blow job to a random delivery guy, because Charlotte's disgust at Samantha's outright exhibitionism during the last episode hasn't taught her any decorum.

Charlotte is too embarrassed to buy her chosen self-help literature at the bookstore, because she doesn't want to seem like the other women in there, sobbing over the pages. So instead she buys it online, receives it, but then decides to throw it out the window because…. I don't know. It's kind of a stupid thing to do, not to mention dangerous because it just about hit someone, and of course it's another shameless waste of money on SATC. She could have at least given it a read and then maybe donated it to charity or something; Charlotte has previously been heard banging on about helping the poor.

Miranda goes to Weight Watchers, and after getting into an argument when the girl who weighs her carelessly records her weight incorrectly, she there meets another chubster, Tom. They have their first date at a café and split a donut, which to me suggests that these are two people enabling each other's addiction and they should stay clear from each other until they have at least finished part of the Weight Watchers program. Instead they (you guessed it) hop into bed in the mistaken belief that a fuck will work off half a donut (see, they really need to attend some of the program so they can learn a few things). It's hard to write about the next bit because it's too gross, so I'll make it quick. *Tom is a sloppy muff-diver and likes to kiss Miranda afterwards*. (This spells the end of their relationship). I can't think about this any more.

Samantha decides to blow her delivery guy, in her office, with the door unlocked, when she is expecting Carrie. She does this so often and it's getting tiresome (Richard under his desk in his glass-walled office, for example). She really needs to find another interest. The public sex obsession is getting old. Later in the episode, she is angry when the SATC girls judge her behaviour, which is both promiscuous and careless. It never occurs to Samantha that she should be the one apologising to Carrie for being such an embarrassment; nor does it occur to her that women in their 40s should have some sort of handle on their libido by now instead of constantly acting like 16 year old boys making notches on their bedheads.

For some reason Carrie decides to let the aforementioned sex addict decide what Carrie should wear on the cover of her ~~compendium~~ book –

and Samantha comes up with something only marginally less horrible than the publisher's own suggestion, which was to be naked. Samantha insists on a fluffy pink hooker ensemble which may have been OK in the 1960s when that sort of tizz was new and fresh. Samantha may have this same ensemble in her hooker wardrobe, but she isn't wearing it on the cover of a book, is she? Why Carrie even agrees to try it on is not clear. She could have just said no; I'm not wearing it. After all, she said no to the naked idea. But she puts it on, we all get a look at it in its full glory, and Samantha is the only one who can't see how awfully trashy it looks.

In the end, I wasn't that excited by the cover, really. It looks like a black 1980's office power suit jacket with no pants. It's the best of three, but I would have loved to have seen a pretty, brightly coloured dress below the knees and above the cleavage. Something a bit eye catching, with a bit of class. But maybe I'm just not the target market.

Questionable Plot Point: Miranda's muff diver taking the whole sheet with him when he gets out of bed. Modesty isn't a key concern in SATC, so why is this guy doing that annoying sheet thing we keep seeing?

5 "Plus One is the Loneliest Number"

Unfortunately Season 5 is an introduction to the angry, jealous and mostly humourless Jack Berger, who ranks in my list of Carrie's boyfriends somewhere in the bottom quartile of likeability. He properly gets going in Season 6. Somehow, Samantha has agreed to work with bitchy Anthony to prepare Carrie's book launch party; although they seem like they would disagree on everything, and hasn't Samantha previously made a fuss about preferring to run entire PR gigs on her own? Samantha gets a chemical peel that has such bad immediate results that she should have asked for her money back.

Miranda is offered post-baby sex with yet another guy, seeing as the muff-diver is now history. This guy's actually cute too, but he's a bit put off by the presence of the baby crying during sex, so he runs out the door as quickly as possible. Which was a bit rude if you ask me. Surely he and Miranda could have taken a bit of a baby-settling break, had a cup of tea and then continued? It would have been more considerate to have dumped Miranda after things were, well, completed satisfactorily.

Jack Berger. Where to begin. The whole thing gets off to a shady start when he flirts with Carrie for a few hours over milkshakes, but then suddenly brings his girlfriend into the conversation. Nevertheless, he turns up to Carrie's launch party to tell her how fabulous he thinks she is, continuing the spark she felt with him on false pretences. It's a shame things don't end there, as we shall see.

Charlotte is confronted by Bunny, her ex-mother in law, at Charlotte's apartment the morning after her adult sleepover with a model-like blonde cutie. Surprising Charlotte in her nightgown, Bunny enters the apartment with her own key. She embarrasses Charlotte in front of Blondie by reminding Charlotte that she is still married and doesn't even own the apartment she is entertaining men in, carefully watched and reported on by the neighbours. (Charlotte really dodged a bullet when she and Trey finally split up, if only for the fact that Bunny was pretty much the worst mother in law ever.)

The thing is, though, why didn't Charlotte make sure her name was on the title of the apartment, instead of just trusting that it was all done when she hadn't even signed anything? Also, why does Blondie care much if Charlotte is still married, considering she is firmly separated? Does it matter so much if you like a person who happens to be on their way to a divorce? Should separated people be forced to discuss this subject as early as on a first date? How long do married-but-separated people have to stay out of the dating pool? Charlotte and Trey's marriage has frankly been over for a long time by now, so I think Blondie could have been a bit less harsh and stuck around for a cup of tea and a discussion, like an adult. He's the second impetuous male this episode and I've had just about enough of it.

At Carrie's huge book launch party, where all sorts of random celebrities appear for no real reason, Samantha turns up after a face peel that looks like she's been blowtorched. Now, I've had facial peels and I can tell you that they don't look like this. There is almost no redness, if any, and the peeling of the layer of skin takes place many days after the procedure. The peeling isn't exactly attractive but it can be covered with enough foundation. Also, at no point is there any pain. It is a pretty simple everyday kind of treatment. So I have no idea what Samantha's doctor did to her but whatever it was, it was a disgrace and Samantha should have sued his ass, because America yeeeaaaahhhhhh.

6 "Critical Condition"

Charlotte finally decides to do something about the assets she was promised by Trey, who hasn't delivered. Carrie bumps into Nina Katz over and over again, but not after this episode. Samantha returns a vibrator that she has almost certainly broken from overuse. Miranda struggles with single parenthood and no one gives a shit.

Charlotte is booked in to see her new lawyer, Matthew Blume, so she asks Miranda if he's any good. This amused me because does Miranda know every divorce lawyer in NY? She isn't even a divorce lawyer herself. I don't think. Anyway, Sir Blume is hot, which distracts Charlotte who somehow doesn't feel she can be herself around him. Um. Charlotte then meets Harry, another lawyer in the same firm, who is so gross while chewing and spitting out a bagel that Charlotte decides she must have Harry instead, even though she is repulsed. This is strangely how she decides what makes a good lawyer. I note she doesn't ask Miranda for her advice about how good a lawyer Harry is.

Samantha decides to have sex with herself (again. I know masturbation is healthy and normal and blah blah but do we really have to see quite so much of it? I'll say it again, she really needs a proper hobby.) This time, her poor overworked vibrator dies from exhaustion and Samantha responds to this crisis by banging it on her bedside table in frustration, because now she won't be able to have an orgasm. I cannot believe she only owns one vibrator.

Miranda is struggling terribly with motherhood (although it must be noted, she's not coping any worse than any other new mother. *You got this Miranda*). Brady won't stop crying and it's driving her to distraction. She receives no support from her friends nor other random mothers in her apartment building: Miranda gets a middle-of-the-night visit from a horrible neighbour to tell her that Brady is being too noisy. The irony here is that the neighbour is also a parent, so she really could have been a bit nicer and less aggressive about it, or preferably put in a pair of earplugs and fondly remember back to the day when her own child did this. Accusing Miranda of being an elevator snob and having no empathy for Miranda and her crying baby, plus letting Miranda struggle with a heavy door and a pram, makes her and all the mothers in the building complete bitches.

And we can't let Carrie off the hook here, either. Carrie calls Miranda in a panic about her book review, and then somehow moves onto her failed relationship with Aiden and peppers Miranda with questions about that. Miranda can hardly stand it (could you?) and tells Carrie to stop crapping on about her own problems and remember that Miranda now has a small human being who she is responsible for 24/7 and isn't getting any acknowledgement from her so-called friends.

So what does Carrie do? Rush over with a home cooked meal, make Miranda a cup of tea, offer to hold the baby for 10 minutes while Miranda has a shower? Hell no. She calls up Samantha, and berates *her* for being a bad friend to Miranda, telling Samantha to get over there and help. Amazingly, this actually happens, and more amazingly, Miranda agrees to let Samantha look after her two-month-old child while she goes to get her hair done. Samantha, who calls babies arseholes, has always shown an obvious dislike for children and has never changed a nappy in her life. If I were Miranda, I'd prefer to let the cat do the babysitting.

Carrie, who is truly at her most self-absorbed this episode, spouting endless verbiage of woe to Miranda, Samantha, Steve and Stanford, keeps bumping into a woman called Nina Katz who's some kind of bigwig at Saturday Night Live. Nina tells Carrie that she went out with Aiden right after Carrie, and pulls "The Face" to convey what she thinks of Carrie. It transpires over the next few scenes that Nina has quite the opinion of what Carrie did to Aiden, and has wasted no time telling all sorts of people about it. Even Heather Graham knows about it! Like she'd care.

But while on the subject of Heather Graham, I must say that I thought she'd be a better actress than to pull the exact same Face that Nina did. I mean; when you meet someone whose reputation has preceded them, who you've already formed an opinion about before you've even met them, don't you just keep that to yourself and smile politely? I think that's what most people do.

Yeccch Plot Point: Samantha returning her exhausted vibrator to the guy at the store who manages to hide his disgust when she hands the appliance back to him, out of its box, knob end first. I am absolutely sure there are hygiene rules about returning certain used goods and he was within his rights to deny it, especially as it's actually a neck massager. Next time, Samantha, buy a vibrator.

Miranda Moment: After using Samantha's exclusive hair appointment at a top salon while Samantha watches the baby, Miranda returns with her hair looking… a little less greasy but otherwise pretty much the same as when she left.

Miranda quote: "I feel disgusting. All of my clothes smell like barf. I don't have time to shower, much less get a haircut." And yet here you are, Miranda, having brunch in a café with the girls.

7 "The Big Journey"

Carrie manages to convince Samantha to spend over 3 days getting a train to San Francisco instead of the mere 5 or 6 hours on a plane, due to Carrie's irrational fear of flying. Charlotte has sex with her future husband despite finding him ugly, and decides to use him as a fuck buddy only. Miranda has much of the episode off camera.

If my memory is correct, Big had actually given Carrie a plane ticket to visit him any time she likes, so why does she a) decide to get a train to LA and b) drop in on him unannounced, instead of properly planning a dirty weekend like normal people? What if Big wasn't in LA? What if he has a new girlfriend? This sort of impulsiveness really annoys me, especially as we all know Big is very particular about lots of things and could possibly find this surprise visit a bit of an imposition. Also, Carrie's fear of flying is based on the security scanning of her makeup bag, which she finds offensive. It's not about the physical being in the air. Can she be any more ridiculous? If I were Samantha, I'd go to SF on the plane and meet Carrie there. I've no time for this sort of crap.

It's a shame I wasn't there to give Samantha advice, because it turns out I was right – three days on a train is some kind of hell and there aren't even any men on there that Samantha would deign to fuck (because that's what Samantha was planning on doing on the train, just for something different). The girls have an expletive filled conversation about sex, men and being horny in front of an Amish couple at their lunch table (although it's really not the sort of conversation they should be having in front of anyone except the other SATC girls. I think they've forgotten how to behave in polite company).

Charlotte has sex with Harry, whom she generally finds repulsive but for some reason can't resist him. She chooses to consult with Anthony Marentino, her bitchy gay friend, for the rules about engaging Harry on a sex-only basis, ie. a fuck buddy. But wait a minute, Charlotte, didn't we go into some detail about that back in season 2, episode 14? Have you forgotten already? Regrettably, Anthony is very practised at being rude to people. He instructs Charlotte to be rude to Harry by saying: "Fuck me, and get out", which she duly does after their next liaison even though he invites her to dinner like the gentleman he is. Charlotte doesn't deserve him, but Harry doesn't seem to mind being treated as a prostitute, albeit an unpaid one. Stay tuned, because it's not the shittiest thing she'll ever do to Harry.

Samantha and Carrie continue their three days of hell on a train, where Carrie gets a huge zit the size of a thumbnail smack in the middle of her cheek, and Samantha insists they crash a bachelor party where they are wholly ignored by the carriage full of uninterested men. They get drunk back in their carriage instead – well, at least Samantha does – where they discuss Samantha's mid-life thing, and Carrie pops the zit. And 24 hours later, the zit has miraculously disappeared, which is the fastest I have ever seen one of those things clear up, especially one of such epic proportions.

Carrie attends her first book reading and even though she hasn't contacted Big, there he is in the audience! What a coincidence. Big has read the book, and is mortified to discover that like the last 5 seasons, it's mostly about him and his shameful behaviour. He's almost too ashamed to have sex with Carrie, but something about a good night's sleep makes him forget about all that and give it to her the next morning. Phew, because otherwise the whole trip was a complete bust for Carrie and Samantha both.

8 "I Love a Charade"

Carrie wears a terrible dress and worse hairstyle to a Hamptons wedding. We are assailed with mentions of "zsa zsa zsu", a made-up term of speech that thankfully only lasts one episode. Berger shows up again, now single but no more likeable. Charlotte realises she has fallen for Harry, but is dismayed when he tells her it can never be because she's not Jewish (which explains why he was OK with being a fuck buddy). Samantha demands Smarmy Richard, who she dumped a while ago, allow her to use his Hamptons house for a huge party. The SATC girls crack continual jokes about Bitsy von Muffling marrying the gayest man in New York.

The girls are off to a wedding, amidst their disbelief and amusement that Bobby Fine, a cabaret piano entertainer who tells his audience he wears pink caftans and a Peggy Lee wig in the privacy of his own home, is marrying Bitsy Von Muffling, a thin middle aged socialite with platinum hair. There is much consternation among the SATC girls about why they are getting married at all, but the general agreement is that it must be for companionship. Carrie bleats on about the *zsa zsa zsu* – the butterflies in your stomach you get when you're in love – and how it couldn't possibly exist in a gay/straight union. I'm already wishing *zsa zsa zsu* didn't exist as vocabulary in the script.

In ongoing coincidences, Harry handled Bitsy's divorce, so he's invited to the wedding. He wants Charlotte to go with him, and as they are slowly progressing away from fuck buddies to something more, Charlotte agrees to go; but only if he waxes his back. He must have it done at the same place that butchered Samantha's face peel, because after the wax his back looks as though it's been grilled on a Broil King. We've all waxed our legs, haven't we ladies? There should be no ongoing redness or welting, and certainly no pain after the procedure. Charlotte is horrified to see Harry's back looking like breakfast bacon, but at least it's hairless. She finds other things to complain about though: Harry's shirt, his use of the word "tits" and his tendency to eat without caring about food on his face. Harry is characteristically good natured about it all. He's slowly becoming my second favourite SATC lead cast member (after Miranda). Except for the teabag thing, but we'll get to that.

On their way to the huge party that Samantha has decided to host at Richard's house in the Hamptons, Jack Berger makes another appearance, just in time to create some drama in season 6. He rides badly on a motorcycle to the very same fast food joint where the SATC girls minus Charlotte are having lunch. It's quite the coincidence. The motorcycle is an impulse purchase Berger made to get him through a breakup with the girlfriend Carrie was hopeful he would break up with. However, he's not very confident in riding it, which makes me wonder how he got his license, and if he should really be riding it up to the Hamptons. Carrie invites him to Samantha's party, and he knows the house because Berger has a Hamptons house as well. (So does Harry; have you noticed how many people have Hamptons houses on SATC?)

At the party, Carrie and Berger sit outside the house together on the grass and Carrie delivers a one-woman monologue about her last breakup and breakups in general, crapping on well long enough to make her seem a dozen kinds of crazy. Berger can't get away fast enough, even pulling his jacket out from under Carrie so suddenly she tips sideways. Carrie, in her characteristic narcissistic way, has scared him off. I'm still waiting for someone to quote Lisa Kirk to Carrie:

"A gossip is one who talks to you about others; a bore is one who talks to you about himself; and a brilliant conversationalist is one who talks to you about yourself."

It may have helped Carrie a little in life. Anyway, moving on to the actual wedding reception. Harry professes to Charlotte that he's falling for her, but then follows up that he can never marry her because she's not Jewish. They decide to just dance and figure it all out in season 6. Miranda is ruminating over her recent accidental sex with Steve (again!) and realises she may be falling for him too. Berger shows up yet again, invited that very day by the groom (because when you pay $500 a head for a lavish Hamptons wedding, it's ok to ask random people on the street to attend on seven hours' notice). Carrie keeps her mouth firmly shut, embarrassed by her earlier verbal haemorrhage, and they decide to date properly before their (spoiler) rocky relationship and spectacular breakup in season 6. Samantha isn't falling in love with anyone, I'm relieved to say, because that's enough love (or simulation thereof) for one episode.

Style note: I can't even say how much I hate the dress and hair combo Carrie wears to the wedding. The other girls somehow always put it together for events, but Carrie is generally relied upon to wear unflattering frocks, like this one that is just a strapless gathered piece that looks like the towel you wear under your arms when you're stripped off and about to get a massage. Don't get me started on the hair.

10 SATC Plot Lines That Remain Unresolved

1. Scout, the bar opened by Steve and Aiden and only seen in one episode. What happened to it?
2. The $30,000 lent to Carrie by Charlotte. When was this loan repaid?
3. Carrie's $4.50 a word contracting role at *Vogue*. Did she ever write more than one article?
4. How exactly did Bobby and Bitsy get pregnant? The truth, now.
5. Did Samantha's sex tape go viral and disprove the public theory that she was a fag hag?
6. Whoever did steal Carrie's Manolos at Kyra's party?
7. What happened to the second apartment that Aiden bought for him and Carrie, after Carrie was miraculously able to buy hers back? And how did Carrie get a loan for the rest of the purchase price given her meagre income?
8. What personal problem did Carrie's ex-boyfriend Jeremy have that put him in an institution for eight to ten months?
9. The smashed TV of Steve's as he was moving into Miranda's apartment. Whodunnit?
10. When and why did Stanford break up with Marcus (so he could marry bitchy Anthony in SATC The Movie (2)?

Season 6

1 "To Market, to Market"

Carrie is way over-excited about her first date with Berger. Miranda suddenly realises she's in love with Steve, which is good timing because it's the start of season 6 and someone besides Charlotte should have a wedding before the series end. Samantha has sex with a white-collar criminal, who is arrested mid-fuck. Charlotte makes the drastic decision to become a Jew so Harry will marry her. There is a rare, almost subliminal reference to Scout, the bar Steve opened with Aiden, but if you blink, you'll miss it.

Carrie and Berger organise a date for Friday night, but Carrie sees him in the street during the day when she's out with Miranda. Carrie freaks out because she "looks like shit" (I'm not touching that) and runs away from him before he can see her, smack into Aiden. In a giant plot twist, Aiden has managed to marry and have a baby, and there the baby is, in a carrier hanging from Aiden's shoulders. Carrie manages to muster up a fleeting interest in the baby, but then tells Aiden that he may have a baby but she has a *date*, which surely has to be one of the most shallow responses ever uttered when faced with someone who's had a baby. (Note: in case you're interested, that was Sarah Jessica Parker's actual child in the carrier, if you believe everything you see on YouTube).

But before this scene, the girls had convinced Carrie that to minimise her nervousness over her upcoming Berger date, she should accept a test date with some other dude from somewhere who also asked her out this week. Charlotte is the one who most firmly pushes Carrie towards this idea, which is weird because Charlotte of all people is most likely to put all her eggs into one dating basket, especially after episode 14 of season 2 "The Fuck Buddy" where Charlotte dated several men in one week and got busted by two of them. But Carrie heeds Charlotte's advice and goes out on an awful date with a nervous dorky guy and only succeeds in making herself even more highly strung about the Berger date. Sometimes the SATC girls just give each other the worst advice.

Samantha invites herself to her sexy new neighbour's apartment and he answers the door in a towel, which means within five minutes they're getting it on. Later in the episode, the FBI bust down the door, where they catch Samantha mid-orgasm on top of her neighbour, to arrest him for insider trading. But really, they could have given the dude five minutes to stop whatever he was doing and open the door. It's insider trading, not homicide.

Charlotte confesses to Harry that she might not be able to have children. He's ok with that. He does need to be a bit careful though, because all this conversion to Judaism/baby/adoption talk is getting Charlotte primed for her next wedding, and she won't be very patient about waiting. Especially since she's discovered that his mother is dead, which lifts Harry's eligibility even higher.

In other plot developments that are about to become tedious, Miranda decides she loves Steve, so picks a fight with him to show him how much she cares. Then, when apologising to him later, she can't bring herself to admit her feelings to him because he now has a girlfriend. Nothing has before stopped Miranda from being as blunt as a bag of wet mice; remember when she seduced Skipper when he was in a relationship because she decided she liked him a bit as well? Miranda describes herself as living an overly articulated life, but in this case, brace yourself: for we are about to embark upon half a season of tortured Miranda angst, as she lets her repressed feelings about Steve ruin her new relationship with the hunky, gorgeous, sexy, wealthy, Robert – but I'm getting ahead of myself.

Questionable Plot Point: Harry ordering pork in at dinner. He tries (unconvincingly, in my opinion) to explain to Charlotte why he could be so firm about marrying a Jew, yet eats pork. I don't care what he says about it; it's conflicted and puts Harry's whole religious argument into dubious territory. I like him a lot, but it's pure hypocrisy.

2 "Great Sexpectations"

Carrie and Berger struggle to have fun in the bed, to go along with their spark-free dates outside of it. Samantha targets her next man but has to fight for him. Charlotte pursues her dream of becoming a Jew with surprising tenacity. Miranda watches television.

During a fun couple of dates and some shopping for shower curtains, Berger and Carrie make out in public until the public is sick of it. Carrie decides to take him home and see what he's got, but she's sorely disappointed. They can hear the buses trundle by as they silently attempt their first lousy bonk, and I can't help but wonder why no one put some music on and darkened the room beforehand - these are little things, but for a first shag they definitely help. Especially when there's no zsa zsa zsu. Sorry. Couldn't help myself.

Carrie whines to the girls about how awful it was, and they are encouraging – Charlotte and Miranda encourage Carrie to give him another chance, Samantha encourages her to dump him.

Carrie does give it another chance, and it's awful again, a fact they both acknowledge. Somehow all they need to do is make this pronouncement, Carrie puts on a pair of fluffy stilettos and boom! the sex is immediately great. I don't know how this happened, but suddenly raunchy music is playing and everyone is being satisfied. All right then. Problem solved.

Samantha takes the girls to a raw food restaurant, which is where the delectable Jerry (soon to be Smith) makes his first appearance. Samantha is so taken with his cuteness that she goes back to the restaurant and downs another whole raw meal just so she can stake him out, along with a dozen other pretty girls and one who looks like a man. She manages to keep chugging down "lawn in a bowl" and cactus entrees until she is the last one in the restaurant, after paying off the one who looks like a man to get rid of her. Apparently this is all Jerry needs to be persuaded to go home with Samantha, although he could have had any of the other girls, some of whom were even less than twice his age.

In contrast to Carrie's lame Berger sex, Samantha and Jerry are pros at first time shagging, and we are treated to another sex montage which includes sex on a chair, on the bed, which I could never enjoy. It looks far too precarious to me.

Charlotte is so desperate to give Harry a reason to propose that she targets a rabbi and pesters him until he is forced to let her join in his family's Friday night Shabbat. And by next episode tah-dah! she's a Jew. That didn't take long at all, did it.

Miranda is addicted to a soap opera where a black man has sex with a white woman. This will have relevance in future episodes but I have to say, I'm always surprised at Miranda's low-brow taste for trash entertainment. The Jules and Mimi sitcom-within-a-sitcom is terrible, with ordinary acting and one-dimensional storylines. But maybe that's just because it's all about sex and we get enough of that in the main storylines in SATC. Don't we?

3 "The Perfect Present"

There's a lot of general angst in this episode, from the SATC girls as well as supporting cast. Berger begins to let his dark side show, not that he was hiding it particularly well. We also discover that Berger needs frog sounds to get to sleep. Samantha has fantasy sex and gets

Jerry sacked from his catering job. Charlotte mourns the loss of Christmas now that she's Jewish. Carrie has phone sex with Big, just to make sure we are all aware of the spark that still exists between them that won't be gone.

So what's with the angst in this episode? A quick rundown:

- Miranda is unreasonably annoyed that Steve is showing what I would call adult responsibility by carrying condoms in a huge sack of stuff for Brady. Surely we all know he's having sex with his new girlfriend, so why does Miranda get all upset about condoms and accuse Steve of being a bad parent? Is it because he didn't use one when he knocked her up?
- Charlotte gets all teary about not being able to have Christmas now that she's Jewish. Charlotte, I reckon if Harry can eat pork, then you can put up a Christmas tree. After all, rabbis don't do home inspections at Christmas time to make sure no one dared wrap a few presents.
- Carrie, not ever to be left out when there's angst going around, is freaking out whenever Berger mentions his ex. The real angst, though, is with Berger's awful temper when he hears a voicemail from said ex. It's a warning of things to come. Get out now, Carrie, and stop romanticising this awful relationship which has no chemistry and little joy.
- A supporting cast member – one of those random friends we'll never see again - throws a purse party (like Tupperware, but selling her hideous handmade purses instead). She's so incensed to catch Samantha having sex with her caterer in the back of the kitchen (it's Jerry from last episode, handing out food on platters, what a coincidence) that she goes absolutely nuts and screams at everyone to leave.

So, in a nutshell, the only one without the angst is Samantha. She does however manage to offend Jerry by offering him money to make up for getting him sacked, which is a bit of a blow to his ego because she offers it right after they have sex. There's something to be said for timing in these situations, and Samantha's was a bit off.

Carrie's phone sex with Big is a bit random, but I concede necessary to bring him back into the series. He's going to be critical to the cast later in the season and in the SATC movies, he so needs to be kept warm.

4 "Pick-A-Little, Talk-A-Little"

It's the episode of faux-pas. Carrie puts the first nail in the coffin that is her Berger relationship, by making a thoughtless, insensitive comment for which he will never forgive her. Charlotte makes a comment to Harry that also does some serious damage. Miranda too, makes a comment that although not successful in this episode, will go on to become the title of a real life and quite ordinary romcom film. There's more sexual fantasy stuff from Samantha.

If there were a list of SATC series scenes that make me cringe, this one would top the list: Carrie reads Berger's newly released book, and decides to pick fault with one tiny detail. And does she ever go to town on it: loudly proclaiming in a smug voice how the scrunchie in the hair of the leading character in the book is so very uncharacteristic of a New York woman, and telling Berger how lucky he is that he has Carrie to critique this incredibly ignorant error on his part. There's just one problem: the book has already been published. It's no first draft. To a reactive person like Berger, who has already shown tendencies to take little things very seriously, it's a disaster. Carrie spends the rest of the episode trying to backpedal like Seinfeld with The Pony Remark. As a writer herself, it is beyond me how Carrie wouldn't have considered her review of Berger's book very carefully before she verbally delivered it to

163

him. After all, she is also very sensitive to feedback, agonising over book reviews and whining to the other SATC girls when they aren't glowing.

Jerry and Samantha role play all sort of situations to ~~gross us out~~ spice up their sex life – I get that it's supposed to be sexy, but Samantha really irritates me when she uses her purry voice and flutters her eyelashes. It's a total cliché and even Jerry seems to be a bit weary of it by now. He'd like to open up a bit to Samantha by discussing his past and his future aspirations, but she's not having any of that – it's too boring.

Charlotte is just as foolish in this episode (her faux pas ranks a very close second on my list of cringeworthy scenes). Firstly, she has already started planning her wedding when she is yet to receive the proposal. She doodles her name with Harry's surname in her Kosher cookbook like she's in high school. She goes off her nut when Harry watches TV on silent during their Kosher meal that she has prepared. She throws out the superbly selfish line "I gave up Christ for you!" as a threat to Harry that he'd better do as he's told because of what she has sacrificed. And most painful of all, she insinuates that she's better than him because he's short and bald.

Actually when I think about it, all this is worse than Carrie's scrunchie remark. I've changed my mind on the ranking.

Harry can't take her desperation and tactlessness, and calmly walks out of her life. But Berger will hang around a bit longer, as there's more drama to be had here.

Miranda learns "the gospel" of dating from Berger, who imparts some wisdom from a male point of view: if a guy doesn't seem that keen, then "he's just not that into you". It's pretty obvious, but Miranda gratefully takes it on board, passing on the same mantra to a couple of girls she overhears agonising over a man who won't call. But instead of being grateful like Miranda was, they are incensed and insulted. The gospel may have never made it past this episode on SATC, but it did become the name of the aforementioned movie, so we can thank Berger for that. Or not.

5 "Lights, Camera, Relationship!"

Carrie nails in the second one on her relationship coffin. Miranda continues to be in love with Steve without telling him, and even sheds a few tears about his continuing to have a girlfriend. Samantha gets all the girls to see Jerry's play, where he appears naked. Charlotte refuses to get back into the dating pool just yet, and when she does, it's going to have to be a Jewish dating pool (which is really going to limit her options).

Samantha offers her services to promote Jerry's struggling little theatre as it presents *Full Moon*, and insists the SATC girls come along to see it. Jerry drops his overalls during the performance and gives a monologue about ... something ... as Samantha would say, who the hell cares. But he is still completely nude at the very end of the play, where we see him from behind lined up giving bows with the rest of the cast. This is completely against protocol: actors do not take nude bows, they throw a nice silk kimono or something on, or their original costume if they have time. Poor Jerry! The humiliation he must feel when the play's director yells at him "NO! You go out there and bow in your birthday suit, or you're sacked!" and he really needs the cash, so he just has to do it.

Carrie receives a huge cheque from her publisher - $25,000, which for a first book is quite something. It's almost enough to pay Charlotte back. Instead, Carrie decides to blow some of it on a new Prada dress (does the word "save" ever enter her vocabulary?) and a new shirt for Berger, who she's dragged along to Prada. He sulkily drinks champagne as she bores him trying on dresses. To explain where she got the money, she shows Berger her royalty check, which in light of last episode when he told her his book sales were flagging and he was feeling pretty crap about it, was quite an insensitive thing to do. As usual, it's all about Carrie. Things go from bad to worse when Berger takes her to Smith's play on the back of his motorcycle, which scares the crap out of Carrie because he's riding it too fast. On the red carpet where all the paps are taking snaps (for a minor unknown production? Really?) Berger is hustled out of the lens by photographers who don't know who he is. It's the last straw for Berger, and like the petulant tool he is, he calls it a night and abandons Carrie, leaving her to explain to her friends why she's on her own. Never mind Carrie. You won't have to put up with this bullshit relationship much longer.

Miranda finds herself decorating cupcakes for Steve's girlfriend's birthday, which Steve had begun to make, but seriously underestimated the time he would need to bake and decorate 20 cupcakes. Honestly, seeing these two in the kitchen is a travesty; neither of them have a clue about baking. When Miranda realises that she is going to be stuck finishing off the cupcakes on her own as Steve rushes off to work, does she calmly finish piping the letters on the cake tops and get out of there? No. She calls Carrie, mid-pipe, and bursts into tears, wailing about how she loves Steve and can't cope with the cupcake situation. (Do you recall Miranda shedding a single tear at the birth of her son? Neither do I.) Does Carrie tell her to pull herself together, calm your farm and just finish the lettering? No. Carrie tells Miranda somewhat dramatically "Debbie cannot have your tears" and tells Miranda to quit it. But this is the sort of irrational advice we're accustomed to hearing on SATC, isn't it. I live for the day where one of the SATC girls tells another to just snap out of it already.

Charlotte mulls over her loss of Harry, due to her own disgraceful behaviour. She remains a committed Jew though, which surprises the SATC girls, as the only real reason for conversion was Harry. You never know though, Charlotte. It might come in handy one day.

6 "Hop, Skip, and a Week"

Carrie agonises over her unstable relationship with Berger, and is unable to let him just go already despite his jealousy, moodiness and general lack of joy. Charlotte faces an onslaught of Jewish mothers clamouring to set her up with their sons, but Harry matches her apology with an engagement ring. Samantha begins her transformation work on Jerry. Miranda has successfully managed to seamlessly convert Magda from housekeeper to nanny to help cope with the single parenthood situation.

Carrie is stuck doing jury duty, after giving a lame excuse to the court clerk who merely rolls her eyes and denies her reasoning. Carrie should be pleased to be called for jury duty; it no doubt pays better than her weekly column.

Charlotte looks miserable as she attends synagogue, helps with charity events and grudgingly accepts offers of dates with single sons of all the desperate Jewish mothers who want grandchildren. One of these dates ends prematurely, with Charlotte organising Carrie to call her up mid date and faking that something terrible happened. She then joins Carrie and Berger on their date, where she can't get away fast enough as Carrie and Berger bicker about carnations and parsley. I can't wait till they break up.

Berger takes matters into his own hands, calling for a relationship break all by himself as they arrive at Carrie's front door in a cab. This is a chance for Carrie to get out, but instead she begs him to flog a dead horse and come up to her apartment to talk about it. Has she no vision? There is absolutely nothing in this relationship that's remotely worth sticking around for – they can barely stand the sight of each other at this point, and the girls can't stand hearing her talk about it. Carrie even hires a car with the intention of driving to the Hamptons to pester Berger into a conversation about the relationship. She realises after paying car hire and driving the length of the driveway that it would be a huge mistake to drop in unannounced to an irritable man like Berger, who would not think this cute at all. More money down the drain to pursue and then abandon an ill-thought out plan.

In the middle of all this there's a flirty call from Big at his vineyard – just to remind us he's still keeping warm.

We are reminded that Miranda continues to struggle with parenthood as she works far too many hours, is blasted by her boss for being late, and never sees Brady before he goes to bed. At least this scenario injects some realism into SATC about single parenthood: it's not fun, workplace discrimination is rife, and guilt will inject itself into every corner of your life. Furthermore, some of your friends will whine to you on a daily basis about the consequences of their bad decisions, oblivious to the fact that you have a baby who thinks his nanny is his mommy.

Samantha turns Jerry into Smith, and then turns Smith into a drink – an Absolut bottle of vodka, to be precise. Smith is mortified that the pose he held while being photographed – naked, with a bottle hiding his groin – is now three stories high on a building. I can't help but wonder what Smith thought would happen when an advertising company paid him a shitload of money to capture his image to promote a huge brand. Once you sign over your image, you no longer own it. If Smith had a problem doing promotional work for an alcohol company because he's an AA graduate, there's no point whining about it now. I, for example, would never pose for a tobacco company. Not that they ever asked me to, ha-ha.

Harry gets on one knee and proposes to Charlotte at the synagogue. Brace yourselves! It's time for another wedding.

Finally, Berger reappears at Carrie's apartment with flowers and a plea to try to make the relationship work. Without discussing what went wrong and how they will fix it, they hug and make up. Berger sleeps over, and the next morning Carrie wakes up to find him gone and a post-it note breakup message on her laptop, which is callous, thoughtless, heartless and so very Berger.

Carrie, in a fit of post-it note rage, smacks the vase full of Berger's cheap pink carnations across the room. It was standing on a round table, above a rug. The force of the blow sends the vase hurtling to land several paces away. So how is it possible that a puddle of water forms *on the table*, dripping down onto the rug and Carrie's bare feet? The only water that could be anywhere would be on the floor, several paces away. #hmmm

7 "The Post-It Always Sticks Twice"

Charlotte flashes her blinding princess cut diamond all over town, while Carrie flashes her post-it note as often as possible to garner sympathy. Miranda has lost all her baby weight because she no longer has time to eat (despite us seeing her at several cafes in each episode). Samantha tells Smith to publicly pretend he's single, but then gets irrationally jealous when he follows her instructions.

The girls head off to a hot new bar called Bed (which is filled with actual beds, what a hoot), in an attempt to pull Carrie across the line in getting over her post-it note. After they find themselves a bed, having lost Miranda in the process - she finds another bed with a cute guy on it – Carrie spies some friends of Berger's over on the next bed. They look completely bored so Carrie decides to head on over to say hello, because if she doesn't it'll "get back to Berger". She really shouldn't have cared about that, because what she does next is so, so much worse than ignoring them. Hawking up her innermost psycho, Carrie lectures the guys, telling them Berger was bad in bed, backtracking on that, and then angrily explaining the whole post-it incident. When they continue to look bored, Carrie then explodes into a rage, advising them of the best way to react when someone has been broken up with via a post-it, as they don't seem to understand the post post-it protocol.

It's reminiscent of that recent scene where she tells Berger he shouldn't have included a scrunchie in his book. It's season six already; time to learn either the art of verbal control, or to say nothing at all. I feel the urge to rock back and forth, muttering "why, Carrie, why" with my head in my hands.

In a cloud of embarrassment, the girls then head next door to a seedy bar to attempt to track down some marijuana, because that's exactly what Carrie needs to improve the whole unpleasant day: a fuzzy brain and the munchies. At said bar, Samantha embroils herself and Carrie in a skanky catfight with some local chicks after she sticks her tongue down the throat of one of their dudes. And why does Samantha act like this? Because she has seen Smith on MTV, telling the audience that he's single. Exactly like she told him to do. And it made her jealous.

Charlotte is giving thought to her upcoming nuptials and is alternately excited and ashamed about them because this is her second wedding. She must be the first person in NY to feel depressed about this being the second time around. The first marriage is just for practice, everyone knows that.

Samantha has managed to score a doobie from someone, so she lights it to share with Carrie (Miranda and Charlotte are wisely keeping offscreen during all this). There happens to be a police car travelling by, searching for people with doobies, and they catch Carrie with it mid-inhale. But the post-it note makes yet another appearance, giving Carrie a get-out-of-jail-free card as the officer takes sympathy on her and lets her go with a warning. Which is great, because the last thing Carrie can afford is bail.

The girls reminisce over their day, and the episode ends with this inane voiceover.

Inane Voiceover: "I might never find the lesson in why Berger and I split. But at least, for the moment, there was a banana split."

I'm guessing this was an attempt at poetry and the writers couldn't think of what to rhyme with "split".

8 "The Catch"

Carrie decides to accept an offer from a NY Magazine editor to write about the flying trapeze (yes. I do find this a bit random). Charlotte arranges for herself and Harry to be photographed for The Sunday Times, but the result is unsatisfactory. It's the first of many problems in the leadup to Charlotte's wedding, who can't cope due to her overwhelming need for perfection. Miranda is so threatened by Steve's new girlfriend that she hides under the bed rather than meet her. Samantha gets stuck in her dress.

To summarise, here's a list of things that go wrong in the days before Charlotte's wedding, and on the Big Day itself.

- Charlotte can't get Harry to smile properly for the Sunday Times photographer, but that's irrelevant because the picture ends up being printed with a Hitler-like moustache on Charlotte's lip
- Harry sees Charlotte in her wedding dress the day before the wedding, which freaks out a superstitious Charlotte
- Samantha's bracelet breaks in the church and spills pearls all over the floor, which Charlotte then slips on
- Harry spills red wine on Charlotte's beautiful white wedding dress during the marriage ceremony (what a putz)
- The best man gets falling down drunk and makes a horrible speech including expletives, mostly directed at Carrie

- Miranda's speech transcript catches fire when she holds it too close to a candle
- The bridal bouquet lands on Miranda's head

But apart from this, all is well. Charlotte is finally married to the second man of her dreams, and it only took two episodes of planning and 15 minutes of episode time.

Carrie is tactlessly set up with the groomsman by Harry and despite being initially hesitant about it, she makes the error in judgement of taking the groomsman home and having sex with him. He turns out to be rotten in bed, and expectant of more action the next day. She turns him down, and receives some severe rudeness from him during the ceremony and reception. She'll think twice about shagging a groomsman the night before she walks down an aisle with him. Maybe.

In other silliness, Miranda can't bring herself to man up and meet Steve's girlfriend, even though as the SATC girls point out, Debbie is heavily involved in Brady's life now. She's a frontrunner for step-parent status if things go well for Steve. So when Steve brings Debbie over to Miranda's to pick up Brady, Miranda actually hides under the bed to avoid seeing her. This is just wack, as Magda would concur, being forced to cover for Miranda's crazy. Debbie has brought Miranda a candle too, which seems like a nice thing to do. There was no need to be offended by the gesture and refer to it as a "fucking candle", was there Miranda?

Samantha gets stuck in her dress and later has trouble getting her pearl bracelet off. She has Smith handy to help her with the first issue but not the latter. I think there's supposed to be a message in there about how Samantha finally realises that sometimes it's good to have a man around. She fiddles with the bracelet most annoyingly at the ceremony, instead of asking, say, Carrie, or Miranda, or any of the guests who happen to be at the wedding ceremony who could have done the job opening the clasp on the bracelet. So it breaks, pearls go everywhere and Charlotte nearly cracks her ankle. It's lucky Harry caught her, or she might never have spoken to Samantha again.

9 "A Woman's Right to Shoes"

We are treated to a bit of eye-candy: Miranda's hot new neighbour. Tatum O'Neal also joins in as another of Carrie's friends that we've never seen before and will never see again (I loved her in Paper Moon, by the way). Carrie is shoe shamed. Harry starts leaving used tea bags all over Charlotte's apartment and wandering around naked – he waited until after the wedding to do all this – which I find particularly amusing given that Charlotte didn't "grow up in a naked house" and so finds this quite improper. Samantha is irritated by children in restaurants, which is a filler plotline if I ever saw one.

Carrie is shown in a montage of shopping expeditions for her friend Kyra as Kyra gets engaged, married and starts having children. At every event, there's a gift register. Even though this is the first time we've met Kyra, it seems Carrie has spent over $2,300 on this woman and her life choices, even though Kyra throws really shit parties where you have to bring a registry gift, take your shoes off at the door and get your own drink, because the host sure won't get one for you.

To make matters worse, when Carrie removes her expensive shoes at the latest shit party, they are stolen by persons unknown and Kyra couldn't be less interested. (If I was asked to remove my shoes at a party, I would go home immediately, taking my gift with me. But that's just me). Kyra eventually offers to pay for the Manolos after Carrie bravely pesters her to perform some detective work on who might have taken them, but baulks at the $485 price tag. Kyra is a wealthy photographer who used to wear Manolos before she started ripping off Anne Geddes. This is one friend I would be happy to strike off my friend list; the most ingenious thing Carrie ever did on SATC was to leave her a phone message advising Kyra of Carrie's gift registry for a single pair of Manolos as a "getting married to myself" celebration. I'm firmly on Carrie's side here. Unsurprisingly and also alas, Kyra doesn't seem to be at Carrie's wedding in SATC The Movie (1), where she would have had a chance to give Carrie some further equitable payback before Carrie never sees her again, again.

Harry is being a total slob in Charlotte's apartment, leaving his used tea bags on benchtops and other random free spaces. This disgusting behaviour is matched or possibly exceeded by Harry's ever-present and fairly offensive nakedness, sitting on white furniture and wandering around the place, devil-may-care. He contritely tells Charlotte he's trying to "watch his ass" around her apartment but I don't really think he's trying hard enough. There is some ass watching, but he's not the one being forced to do it.

Miranda and her co-op board interview a hunky prospective tenant who Miranda straight away sees as potential relationship material plus a convenient source of sex, and goes all giggly like a girl. As he's black, Miranda plays the race card and gets him an apartment in the building by more or less accusing her board members of potential discrimination. And thus sets the stage for Miranda's next relationship; with a smart, sexy doctor who's quite smitten with her, great in bed, and has ~~a huge cock~~ future potential for the life she's always dreamed of. And then she goes and (spoiler) dumps him. For Steve. But I'm getting ahead of myself.

There's more viewing of Miranda's trashy sitcom *Jules & Mimi*, with Robert this time, who surely must find it a bit tedious.

Samantha has food thrown at her by a child in a café, after being snarky generally about children and especially in restaurants. She kind of has a point.

10 "Boy, Interrupted"

Carrie reconnects with her high-school boyfriend, but then discovers a problem. Miranda and Hot Robert start having sex. Samantha gets herself in trouble by impersonating someone with a pool membership. Stanford discovers his boyfriend used to be an escort. Charlotte doesn't get up to much; just a bit of jumping the gun with Carrie's ex and Miranda's hot doctor Robert.

David Duchovny (I've really missed him since the X-Files) shows up as Carrie's high school boyfriend from two decades ago. I'm not sure how he got Carrie's number, but even more intriguing is the hint he makes about his personal "stuff" and how he's sort of in a mental institution. During the rest of the episode it transpires that he has "issues" and he'll be dealing with them for the next eight months minimum, but what I want to know is what are the issues for goodness sake? How can there not be even some partial delving into that? Is he ADHD? Bipolar? Agoraphobic? PTSD? Pyromaniac? I really want to know.

Miranda's Hot Robert gifts her two tickets to a Knicks game but there's a slight misunderstanding because Miranda thought he was going to take her to the game, when what he was actually giving her was two tickets to use herself because as the Knicks' doctor he's actually going to be there anyway. After that's kind of cleared up, Miranda takes Charlotte to the game and the two of them gush about Robert's hotness and Charlotte insists that Robert definitely likes Miranda (just like she thinks Carrie will marry her ex, but you were a bit wrong on that one, Char).

We see some very sexy cheerleaders perform an awesome dance for the spectators but one of the blondes appears to be flirting outrageously with Hot Robert and Miranda is discouraged, leaving the game as quickly as possible with Charlotte in case his signalling has been mixed up in her head. But it hasn't! Robert likes her and they tongue kiss in the mail room at their apartments. It's on like Donkey Kong.

Samantha tries valiantly to get a legal pass to her local rooftop pool, but it's only open to exclusive members. Always one to be affronted when told she's not exclusive enough, Samantha nicks a lost pass from the bathroom in the building of said pool and sneaks in, first on her own and then with her four friends, which is high risk behaviour when you've scammed your way in. I would have used that card very sparingly, and certainly not to bring in a posse with me. Actually, I wouldn't have used the card at all. I'm too afraid of being in trouble.

Stanford rarely gets his own plotlines but this is one of those episodes where he gets more than a little cameo. His cute boyfriend Marcus is outed as a male escort from way back, and everyone finds out about it before Stanford does. The biggest indignity of all is that it was Bitchy Anthony who outed Marcus – the same Anthony who is shockingly rude to Stanford every time they meet. (I still don't understand how they ended up getting married. Every time I see Anthony I wonder how Stanford forgave him). In any case, Marcus is forgiven after he promises he never slept with Anthony. Although, that would have been some plot twist if he had, yes?

Special Note: David Duchovny. What a dish.

Nonsense Dialogue: "Maybe we were better off when we thought less and kissed more." – Carrie, referring to her relationships back when she was a teenager. This philosophy refers to a time of life when there were no responsibilities, mortgages, bills, kids, in-laws or any of the other pressing issues you don't have when you're 19. To put this in your weekly column when you're 39 is baloney.

More nonsense dialogue: "Ironically, it was the sanest breakup I ever had." – Carrie again, after leaving her ex to stay in his institution for another eight plus months. It was hardly a breakup. They had two dates.

11 "The Domino Effect"

Big is back this episode with a heart condition that is only fixable in New York. Miranda's Hot Robert meets Steve under embarrassing circumstances (for Steve) and Miranda meets Steve's Hot Debbie under embarrassing circumstances (for Miranda). Charlotte tries acupuncture to get pregnant, which seems to have worked for Bitsy Von Muffling who's at least 50, plus married to the gayest man in NY. Samantha takes a tumble.

Charlotte visits the clinic of Dr Mao, an acupuncture ~~fluke~~ genius who allegedly managed to get a woman like Bitsy pregnant, who outside of SATC would have had no chance in a million. Dr Mao places needles in Charlotte's face, which is bogus because fertility acupuncture points are in the legs, lower back and especially the lower abdomen, which is where the fertility organs are. Additionally, Dr Mao puts Charlotte into a room facing the noisy street, where Charlotte can hear the crowds and traffic outside, disturbing her ability to relax. Dr Mao is unsympathetic and abrupt with her when she rightly complains.

I'm a bit disappointed that this guy, who probably charges a fortune for his sessions, doesn't have a soothing, quiet, dark room for patients to properly chill out in. Given that acupuncture is supposed to be a relaxing experience, I'm unconvinced of his methods and techniques. He's not doing the industry any favours, either; it's a profession which has many sceptics. I think he needs to up his game.

Meanwhile, Big tells Carrie that he has a heart "thing" and has to go to a hospital in NY, because seemingly there are no doctors or hospitals in Napa. Carrie breaks down suddenly into a flood of tears, which freaks Big out, possibly because the crying looks so fake. The floods of tears appear again when Carrie chats about Big's Procedure to the girls, and again when she visits him in hospital after the thing is done. Big is discharged from hospital and chooses to stay in a hotel before returning home to Napa, so Carrie somehow works out where he's staying without him actually telling her, and turns up with dominoes to help him recover from the operation. I can't help but wonder if he was released from hospital a little early, because later on that night Big's temperature spikes, and Carrie reaches for medical assistance via telephone. Big shows a rare moment of deep emotion for Carrie as she lovingly cools him and watches over him. But the next morning his heart is back to its cold self and he pushes her away, metaphorically speaking. Ungrateful sod that he is.

Steve encounters Hot Robert in the most embarrassing way possible: as Hot Robert is giving it to Miranda (they've both skipped a day of work so they can spend it in bed, and I have to say I'm not impressed by their lack of work ethic). After he interrupts their fervent lovemaking, Steve whacks his nose on the doorframe and ends up with Robert the resourceful doctor putting tampons up his nostrils to catch the bleeding (well, I've learned something here).

Miranda also encounters Hot Debbie for the first time, an olive-skinned dark-haired beauty who adores Steve and Brady both. Miranda falls flat on her face as she approaches Debbie, which is definitely her payback from feeling smug about Steve having to endure Robert putting a tampon up his nose. Embarrassments now over, Steve and Miranda can now graciously concede to each other that they are very lucky indeed to have such wonderful rebound relationships. They are about to say more, but Robert arrives just in time to interrupt them. Cliffhanger! Hold onto your seats.

Samantha bosses Smith around in bed, telling him exactly where to put his digits and with how much pressure. I would find this a huge turnoff but Smith is just about the most easy-going person on the planet so he puts up with it. Later, he tries to hold her hand in the street but she's not having any of that – it's what monogamous people do. She falls into a big pile of garbage and twists her ankle, just as she deserves.

12 "One"

Brady turns one, and has a birthday party, where Carrie is irrationally afraid of the clown. Charlotte is pregnant, and then she's not. Samantha freaks out about a grey pube. Miranda is unable to return Robert's I Love You sentiment on a cookie. Carrie meets Aleksandr, and has trouble pronouncing his name. She also hangs up on him twice. Nevertheless, he decides to stick around for the rest of the series.

Even though Dr Mao had no idea where to put the needles, Charlotte is miraculously pregnant. But in a cruel twist, the writers decided to give her a miscarriage in the very same episode. Why, writers, why? And why make her wait until the first movie until she's pregnant again? Is it a lesson for us that you can't have it all? Charlotte has an apartment, money, a man, and looks. As Carrie might say, should we be entitled to everything we ever wanted or just one thing less?

Samantha, who's getting all the minor storylines of late, finds a grey one in her newly grown pubes. She's horrified, and too embarrassed to tell her cub, Smith. Even though he's unlikely to be perturbed (or even notice it, let's be honest), Samantha accidentally dyes her pubic hair an arresting shade of red, which makes me wonder about a couple of things. Has she gone blind as well, not paying attention to the colour on the dye box? Why bother to dye your whole snatch for one hair, when you could just trim it? Why not just wax the whole lot and be done with it? Samantha seems to buy into the wives' tale that if you pluck a hair it will grow back double, but then we also must remember that she didn't know females had three holes until she became a lesbian. We are supposed to think of Samantha as streets ahead of the average woman in terms of her sexual maturity and expertise, but then she goes and does something like this and I'm shaking my head. There's just no logic.

Robert gives Miranda a huge cookie with I Love You emblazoned on it, and Miranda is horrified, mainly because the sentiment has come way too early for her and she's not sure Robert is the one. I don't know what he's missing exactly, because he seems to be the best match for Miranda thus far. He has a nice temperament, a sense of humour and cares about Brady. He's got an excellent job, one you can really brag about. Her friends like him. He's loyal, generous and appears to satisfy Miranda in bed. He's also pretty hot. (I think I've mentioned that). In short, he's everything most of Miranda's previous boyfriends are not. But this is SATC, so Miranda can't seem to let go of her feelings for Steve. If only she could remember that Steve is a bartender who watches cartoons designed for six year olds! Why hast thou forgotten this, Miranda. Get a good look at Hot Robert, viewers, because he's about to be relegated to past cast member after next episode.

Onto Aleksandr. We meet him at a gallery, where Carrie and Charlotte go to see a woman who has decided to starve herself, shun washing, sit mute on a chair for sixteen days and call it "art", all the while charging people to come and see her do it. How much money did she make? I'll do it. I'm up for that.

Carrie is unimpressed, as I am. I once read a book about art galleries with stories about how art is created and how much it can be worth, even though sometimes it's just one colour on a canvas. Art collectors pay millions for artwork a five-year-old can do just because someone famous did it, and I kind of think it's bullshit. So I can't get excited about a woman sitting on a chair for 16 days. Charlotte introduces Carrie to Aleksandr Petrovski, a very handsome and well-known artist who asks both girls what they think of the "exhibition". Carrie is honest, and Aleksandr responds by calling her "comic". He says this completely deadpan, which turns out to be a red flag that Carrie misses entirely. This man is devoid of a sense of humour. But we'll get to that.

Aleksandr gets Carrie's number from a friend of a friend of whoever (well at least that was explained properly) and he calls Carrie to ask her for a date. Carrie is spectacularly rude to him on the phone, twice hanging up on him without taking the time to listen to the introduction he was trying to make. It's the first time I can recall Carrie actually picking up the phone when it rings – everyone knows she's a call screener, so why answer it now? In any case, Aleksandr persists long enough to embarrass her thoroughly for her inability to give someone five seconds to explain who they are. They later go on a 1:00 am date to a place that serves weird Russian food, then check out the ~~starving woman~~ art exhibition to make sure she's not eating. Welcome to the SATC – The Aleksandr Era.

13 "Let There Be Light"

Carrie decides that the best way to start her affair with Aleksandr is to refer to him nauseatingly as her "loverrr" and Google his past relationships. Steve and Miranda are back together, and Robert does his best to make everything super-awkward seeing as they now all live in the same building. (So Robert does have one small flaw: bad reactions to being dumped for a mediocre bartender). Charlotte agonises over her life's direction and chooses the least interested person she can find, Bitchy Anthony, as her counsel. She decides to help the blind, a resolution that lasts twelve minutes. Samantha is a total whore with Richard while out on a date with the ever-patient Smith, who really deserves better.

Now that Hot Robert is Miranda's ex, he starts to make things very difficult for both Miranda and Steve. Admittedly Miranda and Steve are asking for it when they are caught by Robert swapping spit in the lift – must you, guys? – but I'm disappointed with Robert. He seemed like a grownup. To carry on like he does when running into Miranda in the fire stairs (she's trying to avoid the lift, but so is Robert, ha-ha) is very petty. Robert re-enacts one of their sexy time sessions, and Miranda hysterically runs into the arms of Steve, recounting what Robert said exactly about how no man has ever been in her that deep. Steve's all *errgghhh*! and so are we. Make it stop, please. Fortunately we don't see Robert after this episode, but we are left with a cheerful visual of him entertaining two beautiful women in his apartment. He'll be all right.

Carrie and Aleksandr consummate their relationship, so he's officially her loverrr despite Charlotte hoping for more. Samantha helpfully installs more worry in Carrie's head about how many other women he's probably playing loverrr to right now, which makes Carrie slightly jealous even though she doesn't see Aleksandr as a potential long-term material.

Carrie then feels it necessary to look up all of Aleksandr's past relationships, like this is going to give her confidence and self-esteem. It needs to be mentioned that during the SATC series, Carrie herself dated 28 men – admittedly she didn't sleep with all of them, but many of them – and that was only over 6 seasons. What about the years before that, when scores of other men are alluded to? Was Aleksandr Googling Carrie at the same time she was Googling him, asking the same questions in his mind, feeling uneasy? Yeah, prolly not.

Samantha, oracle of great advice, is invited to a party by Smith, who she is beginning to slightly tire of because he's busy with his career and is younger than her. The party is hosted by none other than Smarmy Richard, so she agrees to go in the hope of seeing Richard; why, I'm not sure. While Smith is playing with his younger friends, who are snorting pretzels out of their noses (actually I wouldn't mind seeing that, I didn't know that was even a thing) Samantha follows Richard upstairs in the lift to a private room and lets him fuck her for absolutely no reason that I can think of. Can't the woman just say no? She has no desire to get back with Richard. She's at a party with her sweet boyfriend. She's not desperate for sex. She feels like shit during and afterwards, especially when Smith is there waiting at the lifts, looking pained. She bursts into tears, probably because she's feeling guilt for the first time ever but isn't able to classify the emotion. And Smith forgives her. I'm not sure why, because Smith must by now have dozens of gorgeous women falling over themselves to date him. He could have his pick.

Charlotte goes to an interview with a charity for the blind with the intention of volunteering. The initiation process involves wandering about with a blindfold with someone guiding her, to live in the shoes of the blind for a while. Carrie does a terrible job of being Charlotte's guide, Charlotte gets lost, and that storyline is duly done.

Carrie buys another pair of shoes.

14 "The Ick Factor"

Miranda proposes to Steve and they immediately get married – as in, before the episode is over. Samantha is diagnosed with the first serious illness of the series. Carrie is overloaded with romantic gestures from her loverrr-turned-boyfriend and decides it's all too much. Charlotte and Harry get food poisoning.

Aleksandr writes a song dedicated to Carrie, which he plays for her on his piano. He feeds her fruit, and lovingly reads her poetry when they are all cuddled up on the couch. She finds it tedious and even complains about it to her friends (I can't help but wonder, if it were Big doing all this schmaltzing what would Carrie be thinking?). She becomes so overwhelmed with all the romantic overtures that she faints unconvincingly in the plaza right before seeing the opera that Aleksandr was taking her to, and can't get it together in time for the opera so they go to McDonalds for fries instead. (If I were Aleksandr, I'd be pissed. He bought her a designer dress and even knew what size she was, for heavens' sakes.) But more to the point, it should be noted that in the first SATC movie, Carrie reads poetry lovingly to Big while they are snuggled up in bed together. He seems to find it a little tedious.

Samantha has decided to get new boobs, but in the process her doctor discovers a lump. It's cancer, and she tells each of the girls about it on the way to and during Miranda's wedding. What a downer, but at least Samantha is being very calm and mature about it, unlike when she found a grey pubic hair.

Miranda shops for a wedding dress, being incredibly rude to the poor salesgirl helping her buy a dress (again, what is it with the SATC girls and shop assistants?) While yelling at the girl, Miranda pauses to tell Carrie over the phone to tell Aleksandr to cut it out with the romance stuff. There's no time like buying your wedding dress to dish out anti-romance bumf.

Meanwhile, Charlotte is trying to control her mild feelings of jealousy about Aleksandr's over-attentiveness to Carrie. She tells Harry all about it, no doubt with a hidden agenda to have him pull his finger out and show her some romance, lest she be feeling neglected. It backfires on them, as Harry's romantic dinner for two ends in extreme food poisoning for them both. Careful what you wish for, Charlotte.

Steve and Miranda are married in a simple garden ceremony, and then have their reception where Miranda suddenly realises she's now married to Steve's kooky mother as well. At least she doesn't live with you Miranda.... yet.

The episode ends with Samantha telling Miranda about the big C, and we realise that it's moments like these where friends can get you through anything. Aw.

Miranda Moment: Telling the girls that she hates all that "wedding shit", in front of Charlotte who has had two extravagant weddings, organised Miranda's baby shower and basically lives for anything pomp and ceremony.

15 "Catch-38"

Miranda and Steve have a crap honeymoon. Aleksandr and Carrie discuss their future and Carrie discovers it won't involve children, a notion she's never considered but suddenly wants now that it's off the table. Samantha tries to worm her way onto the patient list of the best oncologist in town, after giving her current doctor the boot for no reason whatsoever. Charlotte has no concept of what a one-year-old baby can understand.

Miranda and Steve's honeymoon: it's just four long days in a hotel with no television and no internet. No wonder Miranda starts to go a bit nutty and rushes out in her underwear and a coat to complain to Carrie that all Steve wants is sex. I really think they could have booked a more interesting holiday for themselves, and someone clever like Miranda could have investigated the television/internet situation more closely before making the deposit. They could have picked a resort, or something in a different part of the US (gasp!) for a bit of sightseeing.

Meanwhile, Samantha visits her doctor, who has successfully performed a lumpectomy. Is she grateful and appreciative? Not really. During the appointment, she asks the doctor for an explanation of why this happened to her (that is, getting breast cancer). The doctor answers her with a statistically based answer which includes the fact that childless women have more of a chance of getting it. And Samantha goes bananas.

Not only does she mistakenly accuse the doctor of pointing the finger of blame upon her "So I brought this on myself?", but she tells him she's going off to find some "hot woman doctor" (have you ever heard anything so stupid? Does being hot qualify you as a better doctor than one who's not hot?) and storms out of there with her paper cape flapping so we all get a glimpse of her boob (yet again, yawn). Carrie, who has accompanied Samantha to her appointment, thankfully keeps her cool, gently correcting Samantha for her overreaction and mouthing an apology to the poor doctor who looks quite competent to me.

I get that Samantha has just had a major operation and her stress levels would be probably quite high. But she asked the doctor a question, and he answered it fairly. There was no reason for her to act like such a mad cow. She's a woman who usually keeps her emotions in check – the only one of the four SATC women who generally does – so this scene is teeth grittingly difficult to watch.

Charlotte and Harry are minding Brady, who is now about 13 months old. While they are having romantic sex, Brady sees them from his crib. This is enough to make Charlotte freak out mid-thrust, scream hysterically and call Miranda, who's on her boring honeymoon. This not only unnecessarily interrupts poor Harry, who is given a shock in the middle of the ongoing business; it also had the potential to freak Miranda out, who could have jumped to conclusions and thought for a few moments that something terrible had happened to Brady. All in all, it's another ridiculous overreaction from Charlotte, who should have put the crib in the next room anyway if she and Harry were going to get it on and she didn't want to be watched.

Aleksandr and Carrie have an honest conversation about their relationship, in which he accurately guesses her age, then tells her that if she wants children she'd better get a wriggle on because it won't be with him. He already has an adult daughter and the snip, so he's done. Carrie discusses this with Samantha, which for once is the right person if you want to be warned off kids (Carrie's prior chat to Charlotte merely had Charlotte speculating on a vasectomy reversal, not considering Aleksandr's position even for a second). Carrie has never before wanted kids and after this episode, never does again. So she chooses Aleksandr, but there will be plenty of other things to send this relationship down the gurgler (sorry; spoiler alert).

16 "Out of the Frying Pan"

Samantha has chemotherapy. Carrie and Aleksandr have an episode-long fight about Samantha's long-term prognosis. Charlotte is gifted a dog, and decides to keep it, having forgotten the mess her last dog made of her beautiful Park Avenue apartment back in season 2. Miranda and Steve suddenly find her huge apartment too small and consider moving to Brooklyn.

I've never had chemotherapy, touch wood, but I would be willing to bet that it would be absolutely nothing at all like the sort of chemotherapy Samantha is getting. She looks fantastic, fully made up, clinking ice blocks with her friends like it's Moet, cracking jokes and praising Miranda for giving head to her ice block. On behalf of cancer sufferers, I'd have loved this scene to be dealt with more realistically. Even the scene where Carrie discovers Big has a new girlfriend is treated more seriously than this. Or when Steve dumps Miranda because she earns too much money for him and it makes him feel feeble. Or when Samantha has a cold.

Charlotte and Harry have no luck with IVF so Harry puts them on a waitlist for adoption. In the meantime, Charlotte is given a sweet little spaniel from a dog owner who treats the dog like it's a burden because it's not of show quality. The dog will get better storylines than Charlotte in upcoming episodes.

Miranda and Steve are facing a crisis: suddenly, everything they own, including their bed, other furniture, homewares, baby stuff and pets, are all in their dining room and the rest of the apartment has mysteriously disappeared. Instead of having a big clean-up, which I find is a great way to create extra room, Steve talks Miranda into looking at a big old house in Brooklyn. Miranda moans about the distance between the two boroughs (I mean, it's 4.8 miles for goodness sakes) and how her friends will never come to visit her (but they barely did anyway. I recall seeing them in countless cafes, parks and restaurants over the seasons, but hardly ever at each other's places). Instead of putting her foot down and insisting that they make do with the apartment that Miranda (not Steve) bought, Miranda considers the Brooklyn house that she (not Steve) will be paying for. They amble about the place; it clearly needs a lot of work, and Miranda makes her disapproval known to the estate agent, telling him about the work that will have to be done for her to make the purchase and the long escrow period she'll be needing. This is before any contract has even been signed or a price verbally agreed upon. The real estate agent just stands there looking meek and contrite. Ever seen a real estate agent look like that? Me neither.

Yet again, we see an SATC girl being incredibly rude to a shop assistant who tries to help Samantha find the perfect wig to cover her balding head. As he shows her his stock, Samantha yells "No, and No. Do you understand? This is not acceptable. This is bullshit". I'm starting to think that maybe this is just how customers are in New York, because where I come from, you just smile and be polite and the shop assistant will do their best to help you. If you aren't satisfied, you can say "thanks for your help" and leave. It's so simple. Why don't the SATC girls behave nicely to shop assistants? Ironically, the wig that Samantha ends up wearing to the premiere; despite being very clear about wanting to be "herself" and not "trashy", the final wig is neon pink, plastic, trashy, and dare I say, a little mutton-dressed-as-lamb. In other words, it's Samantha.

There's another red flag from Alekansdr which Carrie chooses to disregard: he has a very blunt, cold way of putting things. Although she refers to him as "sensitive" (really? I wouldn't have said that), Aleksandr keeps bringing up his friend who died of cancer every time Carrie tries to talk about Samantha. I'm not sure who annoys me most in this episode: Aleksandr, who keeps talking about the death of his friend, knowing that it upsets Carrie so greatly, or Carrie, who keeps bringing up the bloody subject in the first place. They bicker aimlessly about cancer and friends and dying, with neither of them paying any attention to each other, until he calls her a child and she calls him an arsehole. They are both right. They manage to make up, after Carrie calls him in the middle of the night in desperation, because she has found a mouse in her hair and doesn't know who else in the city is able to deal with mice. They make up, but I'm still a bit suspicious. It's not as bad as the Berger era but it's pretty close.

17 "The Cold War"

Aleksandr continues to be mysterious, cold and humourless. Carrie continues to mindlessly irritate him. Charlotte decides to become one of those dog show people. Miranda and Co. move to Brooklyn. Samantha makes a sex tape, to prove to the world that Smith is not gay and she's not a fag hag.

Reminisce back to season 6, episode 6, where the renamed Smith Jarrod is horrified to see his "Absolut Hunk" poster on a bus stop defaced by some nobody with a spray can. Samantha tells him he simply must be more "thick-skinned" if he's going to make it in show business. So what happens when some nobody in a café is overheard calling Samantha a "fag hag" because she is dating Smith? Does Samantha, tough PR woman who has dealt with much more serious stuff, like cancer, laugh it off, or just maybe have a moan about it and then move on? Errr....nope. She makes a *sex tape*. To prove that Smith is straight and she is dating him. This is what a PR expert does?

You must have a level of sympathy for Smith here. His fledgling acting career is just taking off to new heights, and he's no doubt very excited to think he'll never have to wait tables again. When he first appeared on the enormous Absolut Hunk poster where his dick was "three stories high", he was mortified to think that his mates, entire acting class and

96-year-old grandmother were going to see it. So how on earth does Samantha talk him into a sex tape? It must also be said that a sex tape never proves anything, because they can be, well, staged. Luckily, like many other plot points in SATC, the subject is dropped at the end of this episode and we never have to see how poor Smith handles any potential embarrassment from a sex tape.

Carrie spends a lot of time making out with Aleksandr, while he refuses to discuss anything about his art or even let her (or us) see any of it. I for one am dying to see why he's so famous, but it seems we will never know. While Carrie stands up her friends at brunch (not even telling them she wasn't going to show via a quick phone call, which is especially rude given that Miranda had to make it all 4.8 miles from Brooklyn), Aleksandr introduces her to his awful snobby friends who find Carrie in very bad taste with her weekly sex column. They visibly turn their noses up at Aleksandr's choice of woman. All of this should now be ringing alarm bells for Carrie; she should be hearing them so loudly that everything else is pretty much drowned out. Sure, Aleksandr gave her a key to his apartment, something she desperately wanted from Big. But then who doesn't have a key to Aleksandr's apartment? He even has a posse of staff working there.

Later, just like Big once did, Aleksandr decides at the last minute not to come out with Carrie to meet the SATC girls for drinks, so Carrie recklessly takes the drunken girls to crash his apartment late at night when Aleksandr had told her he was working. She gets what she deserves; the door is slammed in their faces after Aleksandr makes it clear they are not welcome. How could she think for one moment that Aleksandr would be a fan of the drop-in? Could you imagine having those four rowdy wenches turn up at your doorstep while you're trying to get ready for your big Paris exhibition? Of all their fights, this one is firmly her fault. He deserves an apology (but of course, one does not arrive).

In the first storyline for Charlotte's new dog, now renamed Elizabeth Taylor, Charlotte ropes in Bitchy Anthony as her dog groomer to prep E.T. for a dog show. I'm a bit befuddled because the prior owner, a dog breeder and old hand at dog shows, had pointed out that E.T. has a defect and isn't up to dog show standard. Regardless, E.T proves to be the best in breed or whatever they call it and wins first place, even though she has her period and bleeds all over Charlotte's suede boots. The win has a lot to do with the way Charlotte looks at the judge – it's almost as though she flirted with him, using her eyelashes to make him forget his moral responsibilities to all contestants. It's a little… unethical.

In the second storyline for E.T., the poor pooch is let loose in the park by her irresponsible owners who haven't neutered her (this is a pet ownership crime in my eyes) and she gets gang banged by a group of horny mutts. Charlotte is infuriated by her easy pregnancy, comparing it to her own infertility, but she has herself to blame for this; I thought she knew better than to allow her prize winning pedigree to get it up the butt by some bunch of randoms when she was visibly in heat.

Miranda does her best to settle into the big new house in Brooklyn, trying not to moan about the renovations, or her sore feet from the walk from the subway, or the lack of internet, or the fact that the mailman doesn't deliver their mail fast enough. As you've probably guessed, she fails.

18 "Splat!"

Aleksandr hosts an awkward dinner party for Carrie and her extended friend list at his posh joint. The SATC girls decide they are mostly unimpressed by Aleksandr, especially Miranda. Candice Bergen makes another appearance, although it's not clear whether she has ever published Carrie's work at Vogue. Charlotte becomes the owner of

several illegitimate puppies produced by the gang bang in the world's shortest doggie gestational period.

Candice Bergen meets Carrie for lunch, and invites Carrie to a party she's having for some random people. It becomes clear why she invited Carrie to lunch and then to a party: she wants to meet any eligible bachelor friend of Aleksandr's, and makes it clear to Carrie that Carrie must provide. We don't really know how indebted Carrie is to Candace Bergen, as the *Vogue* column is never referenced in any recent episode, but Carrie feels she must oblige and begs Aleksandr to satisfy Candace Bergen with a spare man.

Never has the phrase "careful what you wish for" been so applicable, as Aleksandr beings a "hobbit" with him: a boring food critic. I've never met a food critic, but if they are the 90s equivalent of people posting their every meal on Instagram then I get Candace Bergen's reaction: she's appalled. But there's an important lesson to learn here, isn't there? Just because you think someone's fabulous, it doesn't mean you'll like their friends. Candace Bergen instead spends most of the evening flirting brazenly with Aleksandr, even going so far as to just about ask Carrie if she can have him instead of her. I have to say, they do make a nice couple. Candace Bergen and Aleksandr, I mean.

Towards the end of the party, one of Carrie's friends from long ago, who has earlier been spotted inhaling coke in the bathroom, manages to open a floor to ceiling window fully outwards, overbalance and topple out and onto the street into the snow, dozens of floors below. I can't help but wonder: that high-risk window. Isn't that a major building code broken right there?

Aleksandr holds an adult dinner party as his joint, which means he shouldn't have invited Carrie's friends, especially Samantha. Not knowing how to behave in any social situation, Samantha starts talking about her dildo which clearly disgusts both Aleksandr and me. Even

Carrie looks very uncomfortable, as though she's suddenly realising how coarse Samantha really is. The conversation continues with a discussion about French toilet paper and Paris's bad attitude, then ends with Aleksandr's announcement that Carrie is moving with him to Paris, which was premature of him as she's not yet agreed to it. The girls are horrified, but do their best to hide it until they can get Carrie alone, where they fire questions at Carrie about this potentially stupid decision (except Charlotte, who thinks it's all very romantic. She would. After all, she married a man she barely knew who she hadn't even had sex with. And look where that ended). Carrie is infuriated with the questions, and it culminates in a street fight with Miranda, which isn't resolved by the end of the episode.

Elizabeth Taylor gives birth to a number of puppies and Charlotte forgives her for being such a slut because the puppies are so cute. And they don't appear to crap all over the house and tear up furnishings like her last dog, despite having genetic input from up to six fathers. I hope Charlotte and Harry neuter E.T. quick smart.

Aleksandr basically offers Carrie an ultimatum by saying if she doesn't come to Paris it's over for them. In case you didn't notice this is a (no doubt deliberate) direct contrast to Big's move to Paris, in which he didn't give a crap whether Carrie went with him or not. There's something profound about all this and Carrie accepts his "offer" to leave everything behind and go to Paris. I don't know about you, but I had the strongest sensation ever that it was all going turn to merde. But hey, it's a great cliffhanger.

We still don't get to see any of Aleksandr's art, described as *large-scale light installations integrated with video imaging* by Carrie who must have worked hard to memorise all that. I Googled it, though, to see if I could understand it. Google's not quite sure what it is, either; I got a whole lot of ads for projectors for permanent outdoor installations onto buildings. So I'm none the wiser.

19 "An American Girl In Paris (Part Une)"

Carrie has her last dinner in New York with the girls, despite ending the last episode in a massive fight with Miranda. Big flies in and shits all over everything (Carrie's words, not mine). Samantha makes a crap speech at a cancer benefit. Carrie gets the worst reception ever for her Paris arrival. Big wonders if he should fly to Paris and try to win Carrie over.

Samantha has been called upon to make a speech at a cancer benefit. At least she bothers to prepare it, unlike Carrie with her "where to meet men" presentation. But during rehearsal of said speech to Smith, he booes it, calling it "kinda stiff" – and that's being kinda nice. It's full of clichés, boring similes, and nothing new. Samantha patronisingly tells poor Smith that she knows PR, unlike he who only knows AA.

So what happens? She presents the speech, in a hideous wig, and it is terrible. The audience shifts and creaks; Samantha sweats and drones. Finally, she says fuck, and pulls her wig off. Standing ovation ensues. (That's all it took?) As a PR expert, it would have been so terrific to see Samantha give a fabulous, personal, amusing speech with a few brilliant anecdotes, and THEN thrown off her wig. That would have been something.

Carrie's last dinner with the girls is emotional, and there are tears. Also, it was ruined beforehand by Big catching Carrie outside her flat on her way to said dinner. He tries to tell her he's been thinking about her and him and he made a mistake and … is cut off before he can finish, by a furious Carrie who can't believe Big's abysmal timing. If he had just made this declaration a month ago! Is it all too late? Stay tuned.

Carrie's arrival in Paris is a bit underwhelming; when she arrives, Aleksandr isn't even at the airport to collect her, which is incredibly poor form on his part. She has to make it to the hotel on her own, then track down Aleksandr in the hotel saloon where he is cuddled up in a creepy, sexual way with a beautiful cigarette smoking blonde who turns out to be Aleksandr's daughter (phew!). She is horribly rude to Carrie, giving her filthy looks and speaking in high-speed French while Carrie struggles to comprehend. This is the first of many indications that she is about to become not first, second or even close to third in Aleksandr's bizarre French life. For example: he promises to meet up with her after he's finished spending time with his daughter and then a dinner with some museum people, as if Carrie is just an associate he has to fit into his diary. Alarm bells, Carrie.

Carrie dresses herself in the most ridiculous frock you ever saw for a late supper thing; a massive silk layered ballgown that she ends up sleeping in when Aleksandr doesn't come back for *ten hours*. Compare this to the plain suit from an op-shop she wore for her wedding in SATC The Movie (1). But then, Carrie's fashion choices could rarely be described as "appropriate" for the occasion.

Nevertheless, Carrie makes the most of her first week in Paris, being sure to visit the expensive Dior store, spending money she doesn't have on bags of stuff she doesn't need (she doesn't have a job any more, so what the?). She trips over in Dior, loses her Carrie necklace, is given sour looks by quartets of girlfriends dining in cafes when she stares sadly at them, and is generally left out of Aleksandr's life even as he bothers to notionally include her in some parts of it, because everyone speaks only French. The stage really is being set for something Big to happen. See what I did there?

20 "An American Girl In Paris (Part Deux)"

Could Carrie's trip to Paris have been a huge mistake? Will Samantha get her sex drive back? (I hope not). Will Charlotte and Harry be

parents? Will Carrie say yes to Big, or will she refer him to what she said in the last episode? Do we discover what Big's real name is before the series end?

Last episode, Big meets with the girls, who tell him to get to Paris pronto and rescue Carrie from her misery. They've obviously decided that Big is the lesser of the two evils. Even though they've been warning Carrie to give up Big for the last five and a half seasons, seems all it took was for Aleksandr to come along to prove that she could do worse than Big after all.

Charlotte and Harry meet the parents of their unborn child, who is being put up for adoption. This takes place at Charlotte and Harry's apartment, which seems improbable. I would have thought the meeting would occur under the control of the adoption agency at a neutral territory in case things went pear-shaped, as they subsequently do. The young, impoverished parents-to-be who seem to have become pregnant by accident, tell Charlotte and Harry the bad news that they have decided to keep their baby as they eat a spread of expensive tidbits paid for by Charlotte and Harry. They openly admit that they only came to New York so they could experience the city with all expenses paid; because there's bugger all chance of it ever happening again, especially once their kid is born. What a pair of swindlers. Charlotte takes it all rather well, choosing to believe that God will provide when the time is right. Because God allows millions of Chinese babies to be born each year and then put up for adoption, so they should be able to snag one of those before the series is out. Am I right? In this case, yes.

Samantha and Smith haven't had sex in a long time – finally, we find that there is something that dampens all that testosterone: chemo. We discover this after the pair have had their respective hair bristles bleached blonde at a salon and they are in the change room, together, getting changed after their hair dyes because... I don't know why they would have to do this. In any case Smith decides to bring up his blue balls with Samantha and asks her when she might consider relieving them. His therapist probably wants to know too. Samantha's answer is for him to just bang someone else, which is generous of her. Smith is, unlike most men, really annoyed by this, so she pretends she'll be right again by spring. He buys it. What a guy.

Aleksandr has organised a lunch with himself, Carrie and his ex-wife, of all people. I simply cannot imagine the point of arranging for your new lover and your ex to meet each other and then *not even attend* said meeting yourself (Aleksandr bows out, because he's so busy with his grand opening for the art/light installation thingy). Imagine allowing your ex an unfettered opportunity to discuss you with your current! All they have in common is you, so that's all they will talk about. And Juliette does a stunning job of telling Carrie in a very subtle but completely transparent way exactly what she thinks of Aleksandr, which Carrie finds slightly concerning. As if we all didn't have enough doubt that this relationship is doomed.

In other improbable scenarios, Carrie wanders sadly about Paris on her own, because Aleksandr seems to have completely forgotten she exists by week two in Paris. She spies her book in the window of a bookstore, as part of the main display, which I query because would French readers really be so desperate to read the amblings of a single New York woman in her thirties that they would put this book on a pedestal? And was it transcribed into the French? So many questions I have. Seemingly they are, and they did, and it was, because not only is her book a minor Parisian hit, but Carrie is papped in the bookstore by a couple of bookstore customers and invited out to a party in her honour. Settle down, people. It's not JK Rowling.

On the night of this unlikely party, Aleksandr suddenly realises Carrie exists and uses her as a crutch for his neediness, self-absorption and crisis of confidence by insisting she comes with him to the opening of his art/light installation thingy. I have more questions. Why didn't Aleksandr tell Carrie about his opening a long time ago, to make sure it was in her diary so she could attend with him? Why does he only casually mention it when she invites him to her party on the same night? Why does he not even consider that she would attend this very special event that he's been dedicating his life to for ages; in fact it's all we've heard about? Carrie is forced to attend the opening instead of her own party, feeling the urge to support Aleksandr in his hour of need even though he's been a total shit to her since she arrived in Paris. Personally I would have told him to go jump, but that's just me. The party is held without her and by the time she makes it to the restaurant it's over. Additionally, she's spent the night ignored by Aleksandr at the gallery. More alarm bells are ringing for me and I can't help but wonder when Carrie will finally hear the pin drop and decide this is wrong, all wrong. Soon, people. I guarantee it.

Back in New York, Miranda is dealing with a new crisis: Steve's crazy mother, who appears to have dementia and can no longer live alone. Steve tells Miranda that they will have to pay for a nurse to live with his mother (I just love how all his big financial decisions are reliant on Miranda's income and not his, because he's still only working nights at some bar that is probably not Scout and he used to have a big problem letting Miranda buy him suits and dinner, but all of a sudden he's insisting that she buy him a house in Brooklyn and a full time nurse for his mother. Anyway). Miranda wisely offers to have her mother-in-law move in with them, because even though this will prove to be a major hassle, at least she won't be paying a nurse's salary as well as a giant mortgage.

Carrie and Aleksandr have a big fight, which was bound to happen at some point very soon. Carrie finally decides what her friends knew all along – Paris is a mistake, Aleksandr is an arsehole and it's time to stop settling for this passionless, cold, destructive union. Little does she know that as she turns away from Aleksandr, clutching her broken necklace and a slapped face (which was an accident, I'll concede), Big is downstairs approaching the foyer, waiting to catch her and offer her the words we've all been waiting six seasons to hear: Carrie is "the one". As cynical as I am about much of SATC, this moment is actually quite a relief - finally! – and it's nice to find out his name (John) and that he'll be moving back to New York so he and Carrie can live happily ever after. Until the first movie. And the second one.

10 Unconvincing Plotlines in SATC The Movie (1)

1. Carrie chooses a plain op-shop cream suit to wear for her wedding to Big. I can't help but question this after considering all the outfits she has previously worn to dinners, parties, other people's weddings and funerals. The ballgown she wore to her failed Paris dinner with Aleksandr stands as a perfect example.
2. Carrie reads love letters/poetry to Big, and he's bored. The way Carrie was when Aleksandr read that sort of gooey mush to her.
3. Samantha makes a special effort to watch her neighbours every time they go at it. Will she ever outgrow her sex-obsessed mindset and find something else to focus on?
4. Carrie decides to upgrade to her (free) designer wedding dress, but then teams it with a bird on her head. A *bird*.
5. Big can't go through with the wedding, so he leaves Carrie at the altar (so to speak). Hasn't he had two other weddings? Why is he getting cold feet at the third one? He's had lots of practice. I realise this is the twist the whole entire movie is based on, but it seems so…. weak.
6. Charlotte poos her pants in Mexico. I'm just not sure if toilet humour is what SATC really needs, ever.
7. Carrie throws her phone into the ocean. It may have been a better idea to just switch it off, then perhaps get a new number assigned to it when back in New York, because that's a more sensible thing to do. Especially since…
8. Carrie hires herself an assistant to do her unpacking and organise her life, but try as I might I just can't understand how Carrie would be so busy that she would need to have a paid helper. There was no pressing hurry to unpack, she doesn't receive that many phone calls (especially now that she doesn't have a phone) and returning wedding gifts is no biggie; the registry would just pick them all up

and return them for less than the cost of a personal assistant. I assume.

9. Charlotte is afraid to go jogging now that against all odds, she's pregnant. I think this is the single most irritating story in SATC TM (1). Charlotte will be pregnant for nine months, maximum. She's wanted a baby for, oh… 22 years. She can surely give up jogging for this short time if she's afraid of risking the pregnancy. The hysteria over this particular plotline is something I could do without.

10. Samantha lies covered in sushi and nothing else, on a table, waiting for Smith. He's late home, from work, as he advised he would be, and she throws a plate of sushi at him in response. Samantha. Don't be that girl.

11. (Bonus!) Big writes dozens of love letters via email to Carrie, which she doesn't discover until the last minutes of the movie. Every one of the letters is just copied from a book of other people's love letters. Yet somehow this is seen as the ultimate in romantic gestures and it's all Carrie needs to forgive Big. Wouldn't have done that much for me.

10 Unconvincing Plotlines in SATC The Movie (2)

1. Carrie and her overall behavior towards Big throughout the entire movie. I get that the main theme is to illustrate how marriage has ruined everything, just like Big thought it would, but their fighting is 100% Carrie's nagging as she bosses Big to get his feet off the couch, get himself out to an event when he's tired and doesn't want to go, and buy her better presents than a flatscreen for the bedroom. There are nicer ways of saying things, if they must be said at all, but Carrie really sticks the boot in with her whining. She hits the nail on the head when she refers to herself as a nagging bitch wife, but instead of giving that some deeper consideration, she kisses Aiden in Abu Dhabi instead.
2. At Stanford and Anthony's wedding, Anthony announces that he has been given permission by Stanford for an open marriage, which rather than sounding progressive and free, just sounds sad and lonely for Stanford. Did Stanford get married so he could earn that inheritance from his grandmother? Because apart from that (and having Liza perform *All The Single Ladies* at his wedding), there doesn't seem to be any other reason to marry Anthony. And unfortunately, the plotline remains unresolved.
3. Charlotte is cake baking with her two little daughters, using bright red icing, wearing high heels, and a white silk designer skirt. Which reminds me that I have never seen Charlotte in a pair of pants and flats unless she's going jogging. The skirt is ruined, of course. How about some casualwear for Charlotte when she's parenting at home?
4. Samantha sits in her office which has floor to ceiling glass walls, her underwear around her ankles, knees apart, while doing what she calls "freshening up" her vajayjay. While I'm not sure what this entails, I'm positive that this is something she should be doing in a private stall in a fucking bathroom, followed by washing her hands very thoroughly afterwards.

5. For some reason, Carrie never sold her apartment when she and Big moved into their new shared abode. She doesn't rent it out, either. So it sits there, unutilized, no doubt costing a fortune. I think Big should have stepped in here and offered some financial advice to Carrie who still seems to have no clue.
6. I keep forgetting why all four SATC girls wind up in Abu Dhabi for most of the film; in case you've forgotten as well, it's because Samantha gets the gig to do PR for a new hotel there. And she somehow manages to get the deal to include a luxury package for her and all three of her friends. Really? Is she that good at PR? In Dubai, we see her doing none of it.
7. Carrie bumps into Aiden at a market in Abu Dhabi. Ok.
8. Charlotte gets a cameltoe. This is close to the same level of toilet humour that wasn't funny in the first movie, where she pooped her pants.
9. The four SATC girls sing *I Am Woman* at a karaoke bar, which is even worse than their series rendition of *The Way We Were,* because this time they have microphones and all the lyrics in front of them so they can screech their way through the entire song. P.S. None of them can sing. Where is Jennifer Hudson when you need her most?
10. Samantha, upon having her Birkin bag broken during a scuffle in the market, drops dozens of condoms all over the ground and is then surrounded by a large crowd of Muslim men who clearly disapprove. Samantha reacts by telling them all at the top of her voice that "I HAVE SEX!" followed by making sex simulation movements (ie. hip thrusting) and flipping the bird to the angry mob. I've said this before: Samantha is supposed to be some kind of PR legend, but her behavior so often disputes the premise. There she is, in a foreign country with certain very strict customs and beliefs, choosing to disregard them with her alarming conduct. This is the kind of scene that usually ends up on the cutting room floor as it's likely to be perceived as bad taste. What a shame it didn't.

Epilogue

In case you were wondering, Samantha has sex with 41 men and one woman over the six seasons. Charlotte and Carrie tie with 18 and Miranda is the least promiscuous at 17. It seemed like a lot more, didn't it?

Source: https://www.nydailynews.com/entertainment/sex-city-number-sex-partners-true-new-york-life-article-1.326644

References

https://www.televisionofyore.com/recaps-of-sex-and-the-city/

https://www.satctranscripts.com/

www.ingramcontent.com/pod-product-compliance
Lightning Source LLC
Chambersburg PA
CBHW050310010526
44107CB00055B/2187